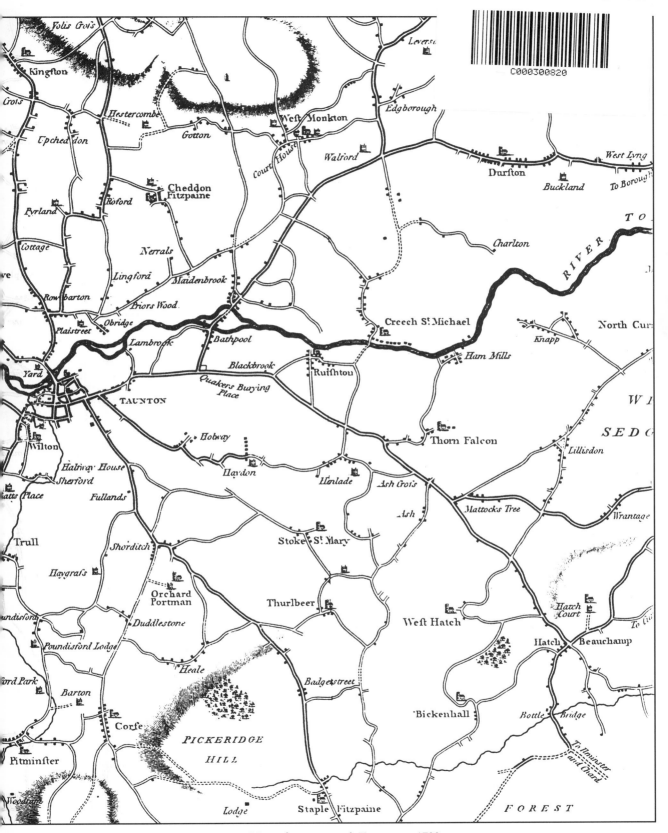

Map of area around Taunton, *c.*1790

THE VALE OF

TAUNTON

PAST

Pepper's Mill, Ash, Thornfalcon, by Thomas Goldsworthy Crump, 1868. The mill stood on the borders of Thornfalcon and Stoke St Mary and was driven by the brook which formed the eastern boundary of the great manor of Taunton Deane.

THE VALE OF
TAUNTON
PAST

Tom Mayberry

Phillimore

1998

Published by
PHILLIMORE & CO. LTD.,
Shopwyke Manor Barn, Chichester, West Sussex

© Tom Mayberry, 1998

ISBN 1 86077 044 4

Printed and bound in Great Britain by
BIDDLES LTD.
Guildford, Surrey

Contents

List of Illustrations

Frontispiece: Pepper's Mill, Ash, Thornfalcon, 1868

Illustration Acknowledgements

Ethel Board, 130; Brenda Bridger, 115; British Library, 19; *Country Life*, 69, 156; Howard Drew, 159; English Folk Dance and Song Society, 133; Gwyneth Evans, 167; Elizabeth French, 53; Mark Gerson, 161; Hampshire Record Office, 21, 40; Paul Hart, 170; Jack Humphrey, 158; Olivia Hunter, 126, 131, 139, 149; Mark Jolly, 64; Tom Mayberry, frontispiece, 1, 3-4, 7, 12, 14, 18, 20, 24, 29, 36, 38, 43, 54-5, 57, 59, 67, 71, 80, 84, 90, 101, 104, 109, 111-12, 114, 118, 120, 122, 124, 128, 135, 146-7, 151, 155, 168-9; Brian Murless, 13; National Monuments Record, 119, 140; North Town County Primary School, Taunton, 132; Private Collection, 125; Somerset Archaeological and Natural History Society, 5, 8-9, 11, 16-17, 25, 28, 30-1, 34-5, 39, 41-2, 44, 46-8, 50, 52, 60, 62-3, 66, 68, 70, 74, 81, 83, 85-9, 91-8, 100, 102, 105, 107, 116, 127, 136; *Somerset County Gazette*, 33, 82, 166; Somerset County Museums Service, 6, 10, 22-3, 51, 65; Somerset Fire Brigade, 113; Somerset Record Office, 2, 15, 26-7, 37, 72-3, 106, 108, 110, 134, 137, 141-2, 145, 148, 152-4, 160, 165; Somerset Record Office (Constance Gray Read collection), 32, 49, 99, 117, 123, 129, 138, 143; Somerset Record Office (Adrian Webb collection), 56, 61, 163-4; Audrey Sparks, 150; George Stokes, 103; Taunton Deane Borough Council, 75, 144, 162; Incumbent and PCC of Wiveliscombe, 121.

For My Father

Introduction

THIS IS A BOOK not only about Taunton, but also the villages and farms in the landscape surrounding it which have for centuries looked to the town as their natural focus. Together, the town and its rural neighbours occupy a large part of the rich farming district long known as the Vale of Taunton Deane and include lands which from the early Middle Ages until 1822 formed the greatest of many estates owned by the bishops of Winchester. The historical links between the town and its setting are unusually strong, and one major purpose of this book is to show how those links have shaped the history of the Vale over many hundreds of years.

The book owes much to that long line of Taunton historians which begins with the remarkable Dr Joshua Toulmin, friend of Coleridge and Joseph Priestley and author in 1791 of the pioneering *History of the Town of Taunton*. In the 20th century, three names are pre-eminent: T.J. Hunt's meticulous scholarship transformed understanding of the medieval town and of the bishopric estate in Taunton Deane; Reginald Hedworth Whitty's unpublished study of Taunton under the Tudors and Stuarts, completed in 1938, has remained almost unknown but is a fundamental source; and during the last 25 years, Robin Bush, in a series of books and other studies, has used his great gifts as a documentary researcher to illuminate many aspects of Taunton's past. I am particularly indebted to the work of these three historians, and also gratefully acknowledge the help given by other historians and writers, including Dr. Robert Dunning and Mary Siraut, who allowed me to see unpublished material for the *Victoria County History*, and Janet Tall, who made available material for her study of 19th-century Somerset agriculture. In addition, Dr. Harold Fox and Dr. Chris Thornton provided a summary of their important research on the medieval manor of Taunton Deane; Mark McDermott kindly supplied a copy of his forthcoming edition of 16th-century Trull churchwardens' accounts; Tony Woolrich shared his knowledge of Victorian Taunton; and Eric Saffin has allowed me to draw on his evocative reminiscences of Taunton in wartime. Material from my own short study of the Portman family has been used in revised form as part of chapter 5.

I am grateful for the outstanding helpfulness of my friends and colleagues at the Somerset Record Office, especially Adam Green, the County Archivist, and his predecessor Derek Shorrocks. At the Somerset Studies Library David Bromwich has as always been a generous and knowledge-able guide, and at County Hall Bob Croft and Chris Webster introduced me to the Sites and Monuments Record. To Steve Minnitt of the County Museums Service and to Colin Clements I am especially grateful for answering my questions about the archaeology of Taunton, and for other help given over a long period I also wish to record my thanks to Lt. Col. M.V. McArthur, Miss L.C.E. Chalk, Graham Salter, Bill and Ethel Board, Beryl, Alistair and Mark Jolly, Rosemary Dunhill, Sarah Lewin, Linda Champ, Bruce Watkin, Ian Giles and Philip Marke. In gathering illustrations for the book I have been helped particularly by the Somerset Archaeological and Natural History Society, Geoff Hall of the *Somerset County Gazette*, Olivia Hunter, Constance Gray Read, Adrian Webb and Rosemary Pease, as well as by QPC Photography and Richard Sainsbury of Delmar Studios.

Finally, I am grateful to the staff at Phillimore for their patience and skill, and to my family for their continuing encouragement.

Cherry Grove,
Taunton
October, 1998

1

Origins

THE GREAT VALE of Taunton Deane, seen distantly from Wills Neck or the lower Quantock slopes, is not easy to forget. A landscape both spectacular and serene reaches south to the long line of the Blackdown Hills, west to the Brendon foothills, and east, beyond the towers and spires of Taunton itself, to the levels of central Somerset. This is the 'paradise of England' described by John Norden in 1609, the land of meadows, orchards and 'rich redd earth' which Thomas Gerard discovered a generation later, the 'golden vale' so often praised by sentimental Victorians. Though the fertility of Taunton Deane was exaggerated into legend, its beauty was beyond doubt; and few were inclined to criticise the innocent pride of local people when they were heard to boast: 'I was bore at Taunton Deane; where should I be bore else?'

Both geography and history define the Vale. Geographically, it covers some sixty square miles within the shelter of its surrounding hills, and extends to the point beyond Creech St Michael and Durston where the Somerset Levels begin. The River Tone, which rises at Beverton Pond in the Brendons, enters the Vale near Kittisford and flows east through Bradford and Taunton to meet the River

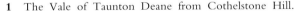

1 The Vale of Taunton Deane from Cothelstone Hill.

2   The River Tone and the late medieval bridge at Bradford on Tone, *c.*1905.

Parrett at Burrow Bridge. Alluvium borders the Tone and its major tributaries, such as the Hillfarrance Brook, but the distinctive red-brown loam which covers much of the Vale is the real source of the area's agricultural fame. This soil rests on gravel, which in its turn overlies Keuper Marl and Keuper Sandstone. The best land, between Bishops Lydeard and Rich's Holford, is a deep, well-drained sandy soil, as good as the best in England. The worst land, at the south-eastern corner of the Vale near Thurlbear and West Hatch, is intractable clay resting on a distinct Lower Lias formation. This was the area where for centuries impoverished limeburners gained a living amid the smoke of reeking lime kilns.

History defines the Vale less expansively, and connects it above all with the hundred and manor of Taunton Deane, acquired by the bishops of Winchester from the 10th century onwards. The lands which produced so princely an income for the bishops were centred upon Taunton and its immediately surrounding villages and form a primary focus of this book. But the wider area over which the bishops exercised at least nominal lordship amounted to more than 40,000 acres. Little wonder that Taunton has been called 'the classical example of colossal manors', or that the manors of Wellington and Bishops Lydeard, which belonged to the bishops of Bath and Wells, and the manor of Milverton, which at the time of Domesday belonged to the king, were overshadowed throughout the Middle Ages by their mighty Winchester neighbour.

HUMAN ACTIVITY over this landscape reached already into distant
prehistory before the Vale became a place for
permanent settlement. Hunters of the Palaeo-
lithic period were probably seasonal visitors to
the Tone and Parrett valleys, using the area as
a hunting ground at least 200,000 years ago.
At a much later time, when the retreat of the
last Ice Age had given way to dense woodland
cover, Mesolithic hunters exploited the Vale
in their turn. In 1951, large quantities of
Mesolithic flint and chert implements were
discovered at Fideoak Park in Bishops Hull,
lying undisturbed on the chipping floor
where they had been made 9,000 years
earlier.

Only very slowly does such fragmentary
evidence give way to larger and more coherent

patterns. The key site for the Vale, and perhaps
for a much wider area, is the low hill which
rises near the church at Norton Fitzwarren.
Tradition would later connect the hill with a
fearsome dragon which ravaged the countryside, and which may be the devouring monster
depicted on Norton's wonderful chancel screen.
The real history of the Norton site is hardly
less remarkable. People of the Mesolithic and
Neolithic periods certainly knew the hill, as
their flint and chert implements have survived
to testify. It has even been suggested that by
the late Neolithic period, some 4,000 years
ago, the hill was the focus of a ritual landscape,
and that a large henge monument, 60 metres
in diameter, stood nearby. Air photography
shows its possible traces a short distance to the
north.

3 & 4 Carvings on the chancel screen of All Saints' Church, Norton Fitzwarren, reputedly showing the
dragon of Norton hill fort. The screen incorporates the name of Raphe Harris, a churchwarden who died
in 1509.

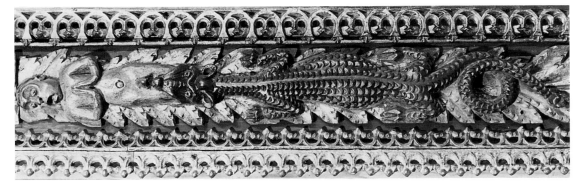

Norton's significance is confirmed beyond all doubt, however, by occupation evidence from the Middle Bronze Age, some 3,500 years ago. At about that time, the hill top became the site for a carefully-designed enclosure, surrounded by a bank and ditch and occupying about five acres. The enclosure, which is nationally rare, was not originally built for defence, since its ditch lay on the inside. It may instead have been used as a ceremonial site or as a trading centre on the frontier lands between tribal areas lying to east and west. Whatever its significance, the enclosure was the work of a complex and hierarchical society, whose sophisticated skills were expressed not least in the production of bronze tools and weapons and of elaborate bronze ornaments. Norton yielded fragments of eight bronze bracelets of the highest quality together with two palstaves

and a socketed axe. At Taunton, Sherford, Milverton and elsewhere other Bronze-Age hoards and metalwork finds testify to a widespread presence in the Vale, and probably reflect communities which to an increasing extent were both settled and agricultural. Of Bronze-Age people in death we have the striking evidence of the many round barrows which survive on the Quantock and Blackdown hills, especially in the barrow cemeteries at Cothelstone Hill and Otterford. Air photography suggests that such barrows once also existed in the Vale itself. Possible examples have been found at Norton Fitzwarren and Creech St Michael; and when, in the ninth century, Saxon surveyors were describing a boundary near Edgeborough Farm in Staplegrove, a *beorh* (possibly in this case a barrow) still provided them with a useful landmark.

5   Excavations on the western side of Norton hill fort, 1908. The excavations, directed by Harold St George Gray, located Bronze-Age pottery underlying Iron-Age pottery.

6 Part of a Middle Bronze-Age hoard found at Taunton Workhouse in 1877.

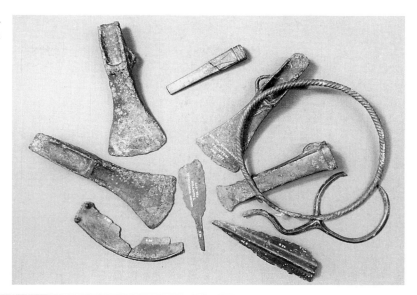

7 Early Bronze-Age round barrow near School Farm, Otterford. The parish contains two groups of barrows collectively known as Robin Hood's Butts.

I N THE EIGHT CENTURIES before the Roman conquest of Britain in A.D. 43, the late Bronze Age and the Iron Age added to the landscape some of its most enduring man-made features. These probably included a system of tracks and other routes which succeeding generations would modify but never entirely replace, and territorial boundaries which may in many cases have been adopted later as the limits of medieval estates. More conspicuously ancient are the great hill forts so characteristic of a period increasingly familiar with war. On the hill top at Norton, Late Bronze-Age inhabitants seem to have created a defensive timber enclosure, associated with the remains of sword moulds, and during the succeeding Iron Age the whole site was made into a full-scale hill fort surrounded by a bank and ditch. Other hill forts rose at Wiveliscombe and, it seems likely, on a commanding spur of the Blackdown Hills at Castle Neroche. The massive embankment of an unfinished fort has

8 Castle Neroche, Staple Fitzpaine, by W.W. Wheatley, *c*.1848. The site, now heavily wooded, is dominated by the motte of a Norman castle, but is enclosed by an outer rampart (partly destroyed) which may be of Iron-Age date.

9 Holway Farm, near Taunton, by Harry Frier, *c*.1890. A Romano-British farm was discovered a short distance to the south in 1971. The field names 'floors' and 'pantile' which occur close to Holway Farm may indicate the presence of a high-status Romano-British building, as yet undiscovered.

recently been discovered above Netherclay Farm in Orchard Portman, and air photography has confirmed another site at Castleman's Hill in Trull. There, a spur of high ground which looks west over the Vale was defended from behind by two large ditches. Traces of pre-historic fields near the site at Trull are a reminder that the Iron-Age forts of Taunton Deane had their place in a landscape filled with people and with their farms. Air photographs suggest that a number of small enclosures, with associated fields, lay next to the road from the Cross Keys to Bishops Lydeard, and similar evidence is also plentiful at Cheddon Fitzpaine and West Monkton.

The Iron-Age farmers of settlements such as these were the inhabitants encountered by Britain's Roman invaders when they turned westward at some time before A.D. 49. The Roman fort at Nunnington Park, Wiveliscombe, seems to date from the years of conquest or immediately after, and a military camp on a smaller scale may possibly have existed near Montys Court in Norton Fitzwarren. From Roman centres at Bath and Ilchester a network of roads soon reached into the countryside, fostering the establishment of large Roman villas and associated farms. But in West Somerset and the Vale, a long-term Roman presence has been much more difficult to find. It is true that the field names 'floor' or 'floors', which occur at Nailsbourne, Holway and Bishops Hull, have led elsewhere to the discovery of mosaic pavements belonging to high-status Roman villas; and it is not impossible that a villa somewhere near Taunton presided over a large Roman estate containing many dependent farms. But no such villa has ever come to light, even though the presence of native farmers in the Roman period has long been evident. At Holway in the 19th

10   Part of a hoard of late fourth-century Roman silver coins found at Holway in 1821. Shown here are coins of the emperors Arcadius, Magnus Maximus, Theodosius, Gratian, Valens, and Valentinian I.

century, stray finds of Roman coins were so common that it was not unusual 'to observe many of the labourers ... wearing a bunch of them attached to their watch chains'. But not until 1971 did rescue archaeologists at last discover a Romano-British native settlement near Holway Farm, lying directly in the path of the proposed M5 motorway.

This settlement was not established on a new site, but probably succeeded a small Iron-Age complex discovered nearby. A large curving ditch surrounded the farm and enclosed an area about 160 metres long and at least 50 metres wide. Within the enclosure, the clearest evidence of human occupation was provided by post-holes which had supported timber buildings of the second to fourth centuries. There were quantities of coarse pottery, a corn drier or malt kiln, iron work and animal bones, and many bronze coins: for though the settlement was isolated from Roman centres and in most respects the supplier of its own needs, it was also part of a trading community.

The building of the motorway revealed a similar Romano-British farm at Poundisford in Pitminster on a site which contained evidence not only of an earlier Iron-Age presence, but of Bronze-Age occupation as well. At Cheddon Fitzpaine a settlement site near Maidenbrook Farm was discovered more recently, and from Cade's Farm at Wellington has come evidence of a Romano-British pottery production site dating from the second to third centuries. Of Taunton itself in the Roman period there is not a sign, though another Romanised farm probably existed nearby: excavations in the 1970s at the Priory Barn and in Corporation Street found evidence of Roman field boundaries.

The abandonment of such settlements in the late fourth or early fifth centuries is part of the larger history of Romano-British decline at that period. Social and political disruption, its causes little understood, affected the country from within, while foreign raiders became an increasing threat from without. The money

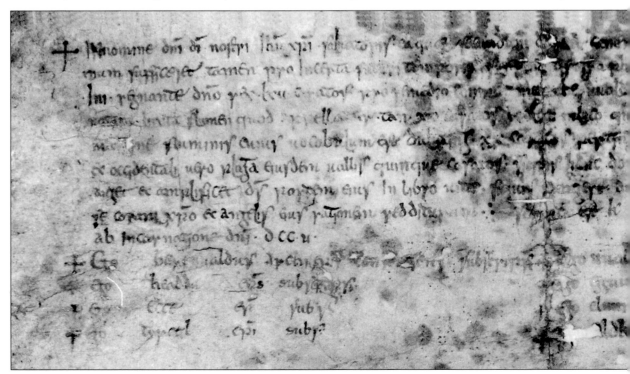

economy collapsed, and many farmers in the early fifth century chose to bury their capital, perhaps in the face of some immediate threat. Any hopes that there may have been for a return to Roman stability were never fulfilled, and numerous coin hoards, including examples from Holway, North Curry and Milverton, were never retrieved by their owners. Amidst so much that is speculation, this, at least, is clear: that by the early years of the fifth century the farms at Holway and Poundisford were deserted, and the landscape around had entered a period of obscurity from which it would not quickly re-emerge.

FOR MORE than two centuries the silence is unbroken, and the occupation of the Vale, which must have continued even without the benefits of Roman government, has left hardly a trace. It may be, as Michael Costen suggests, that settlements bearing the place-name 'Wick' (of which examples survive at Bishops Lydeard and Norton Fitzwarren) are vestiges from the Romano-British landscape. But only in the early pages of the Anglo-Saxon Chronicle, unreliable though it is, do Somerset and the Vale finally emerge into the light of recorded history.

The Saxon newcomers who arrived in post-Roman Britain came first as mercenaries, then as invaders, and in the course of the sixth century may have won the heartlands of the south. In the century which followed, the Chronicle speaks of a determined advance into the region later called Somerset. A battle mentioned under the year 658, and placed by tradition at Penselwood, forced back the native British as far as the Parrett; a further defeat recorded for 682 may have driven them beyond the Quantock Hills 'as far as the sea'. When, in about the same year, a Saxon king granted land at Creech St Michael and West Monkton to the abbot of Glastonbury, none could doubt that the Vale's future was as part of Saxon territory.

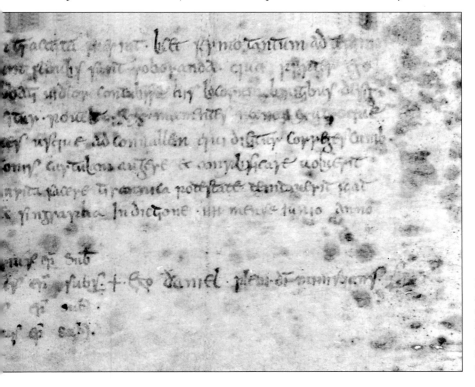

11 Charter reputedly dated A.D. 705, whereby Ine, King of the West Saxons, granted land next to the River Tone and elsewhere in the county to Beorhwald, abbot of Glastonbury.

12   The River Tone and the lower slopes of Creechbarrow Hill, *c.*1905.

The Saxons may have found few oppor-tunities to transform a landscape in which human settlement and farming activity were already so long established. But in one major respect their presence has left a distinctive mark: the map of the county contains hundreds of names which the Saxons gave to their new homes. In Taunton Deane not only do most hamlets and villages bear Saxon names, but many farms and fields as well, suggesting that the early period of Saxon settlement, like the pattern that preceded it, was marked by a wide scattering of isolated farms and very small communities.

Many Anglo-Saxon names are simple geographical descriptions: Milverton is 'the settlement by the mill ford'; Bradford 'the broad ford' over the River Tone; Cheddon evidently 'the wooded valley'; and Ruishton 'the settlement where rushes grow'. Other names are more specifically informative: Galmington was 'the settlement inhabited by

rent-paying tenants'; Preston in Milverton 'the settlement belonging to the priests'; while the many names containing the elements 'ley' or 'leigh' (including Tidley, Ruttersleigh, Angersleigh, Howleigh, Budleigh and Bickley) mark the former locations of enclosed wood-land or woodland clearings. That the names used by Somerset's Celtic, or Old Welsh, inhabitants have been so thoroughly swept away suggests that the Saxons arrived in large numbers and included many peasants who farmed the land. Even so, a few names in the Vale point to a continuing Celtic presence. Walford in West Monkton is an Anglo-Saxon name evidently meaning 'the ford used by the Welsh'; and in the grant of land at Creech St Michael and West Monkton, mentioned already, one of the landmarks is described as 'the hill which in the British language is called *cructan* ('fire hill'), but among us *crycbeorh* (Creechbarrow)'.

Creechbarrow Hill, one of the first recorded landscape features in western England, brings us back to Taunton and the Tone. The names 'Taunton', 'Tone' and *cructan* are all related through the Old Welsh word *tan*, meaning 'fire'. Taunton is clearly 'the settlement on the Tone or Tan' and took the first part of its name from the river. But the river may have been named either from the 'fire hill' at Creechbarrow, past which it flows, or from the fire-like or sparkling appearance of its waters. There are also less likely solutions to the puzzle, but no answer is certain.

THE ANGLO-SAXON CHRONICLE itself first mentions Taunton's existence, noting under the year 722 that 'Queen Aethelburh destroyed Taunton which King Ine had built'. That was an inauspicious start to the town's recorded history, but enough to suggest Taunton's dominance over the landscape in which it stood, and its importance for the West Saxon royal house. What Ine had built, and what his queen destroyed, was probably a defensive position to secure newly-conquered lands and to dominate the chief route westward. It is impossible to say

why this defensive phase in Taunton's early history ended so abruptly in 722, even if one medieval writer spun the few tentative facts into a colourful story. It seems clear only that Taunton continued to exist even when it had ceased to serve as a military stronghold and that its position as chief place of the Vale was unchallenged.

Taunton in the eighth century was above all a royal centre, providing an occasional base for West Saxon kings, but serving most of all as the administrative and religious focus of a great royal estate. The boundaries of that estate may have reflected the boundaries of one or more Roman predecessors, and may possibly have encompassed the whole of the Vale, including Wellington and Milverton, together with lands on the Quantocks and the Blackdowns. The organised forces of Christianity were quick to arrive in Anglo-Saxon Taunton, tradition recording that Queen Frithogyth founded a minster church there during the first half of the eighth century. The discovery of Anglo-Saxon burials on Castle Green strongly suggests that the minster stood close by, perhaps in association with the earliest buildings of royal administration in the area of Taunton Castle.

13 Anglo-Saxon skeleton found under the former coin room of Taunton Castle in 1972. The skeleton's legs were truncated by a 13th-century wall, and radiocarbon dating of an adjacent burial supported a pre-Conquest origin.

As was the Saxon custom, the minster became mother church of the wide territory in which it stood and was home for a group of missionary priests. It was they who assumed pastoral responsibility for the communities of the Vale, travelling out to minister and preach, and they who in the course of time encouraged the foundation of daughter churches. There is late Saxon masonry at St George's, Wilton, to show that at least one of the daughter churches had risen in stone before the Norman Conquest, and it seems likely that many other of the Vale's churches existed in permanent form by the end of the 10th century. There must, for example, have been a church at Pitminster when the settlement was first recorded in the year 938; for its name evidently means 'the church of Pippa's people'. And the church at Milverton was probably already long established when Domesday Book first recorded it in 1086.

The churches of Taunton Deane took their place in a countryside filled with sites of religious significance. Wellington may derive its name from a pagan holy place (or *weoh*) already venerated when the Saxons arrived there. The 'ashtree which the ignorant call sacred' is recorded on the borders of Halse and Milverton by a ninth-century charter, and sacred springs or streams were very common. The same charter records the *halgan wylle* or holy spring which still exists on the eastern edge of Stoke St Mary, and among many other holy springs which survive locally are those at Halse, Thorne St Margaret and near Castle Neroche. St Agnes' Well at Cothelstone, 'the

14   *Below left*. Long-and-short work at St George's Church, Wilton, evidently marking the west end of an aisle-less Anglo-Saxon church.

15   *Below right*. St Agnes' Well, Cothelstone. The well lies close to Cothelstone Manor House and is enclosed in a stone building probably of late medieval date.

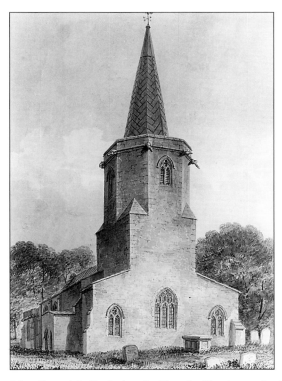

16 *Above left*. St Andrew's Church, Pitminster, by J.C. Buckler, 1832. The building shown here is largely of the 13th to 15th century, but its origins are probably far earlier.

17 *Above right*. St John's Church, Wellington, by J.C. Buckler, 1843. The pagan holy place, or *weoh*, from which Wellington is thought to derive its name may have stood on or near the site of the church.

most beautiful of the holy wells of Somerset', is just one example of such a site acquiring an explicitly Christian identity, a process which can also be traced at Wilton, 'the settlement by the well or spring'. There, a pagan spring, later dedicated to St George, was evidently Christianised in the Anglo-Saxon period and inspired the siting of Wilton's Anglo-Saxon church. Pagan hill-top shrines may also on occasion have been chosen later as sites for Christian churches, as was possibly the case with the hill-top churches at Curland and West Buckland.

The minster soon presided over both the religious life of the area and over a landed estate which was growing rapidly. For its worldly wealth the minster had West Saxon kings to thank. In 737 King Aethelheard granted a stock farm at Withiel Florey and salt pans at 'Cearn'; and in about 854 a generous gift from King Aethelwulf added Stoke St Mary, Orchard Portman, and the hill lands of Corfe. Such transactions mark the process by which the West Saxon royal house gradually gave up direct control of the Vale to loyal churchmen, retainers and secular lords. Sometimes the estates thus granted were very small: Angersleigh, an island of territory extending to about 400 acres, was probably carved out of the surrounding estate for the benefit of an unknown Anglo-Saxon thegn; at Stoke St Mary, land called *knictebare* (later 'Knightsbeer') may identify an area of woodland given up by a West Saxon king to one or more of his

18 St Mary's Church, West Buckland. The existing church contains work of the 13th century and later, and has a west tower for which money was left in 1509. St Mary's was dependent on the church at Wellington at least as early as 1234.

retainers; and at Creech St Michael the hamlet called Charlton (probably 'the settlement of the free peasants or ceorls') may have had similar origins.

The most vivid fragments of the district's early history are preserved in Anglo-Saxon land charters with reputed dates from the eighth to 11th centuries. Boundary surveys of the lands concerned are often included in the charters; and although such surveys can tell us nothing of farmers and their families in the Anglo-Saxon Vale, they do provide a remarkable account of the physical landmarks which defined the setting for those unknown lives. Trees, ditches, hills and brooks are prominent among landmarks which the surveys name, and when likely locations are established today by work in the field and with maps, the results form a dramatic illustration of the debt owed by the modern landscape to the distant past.

The boundaries of the minster's ninth-century estate at Stoke St Mary, for example, corresponded almost exactly with the parish boundaries which survived a thousand years later. Landmarks included the 'ricges' or ridge, now Stoke Hill, and the great bank and ditch which still run unbroken for a mile on the parish's southern border. Another survey describes the boundary ditch which probably gave a name to Shoreditch, and further south, on the borders of Corfe and Pitminster, lay the Grey Stone, the Common Hill, and the Oxen Field. Landmarks on the hills above Corfe and West Buckland suggest the existence of heavy

19 A page from the Codex Wintoniensis, a 12th-century manuscript containing copies of charters granted to Winchester, 688-1048. The first paragraph records ninth-century boundaries and land grants at Ruishton, Nynehead, Stoke St Mary, Hestercombe, and Kingston St Mary. The second paragraph describes the boundaries of the whole of the great pre-Conquest estate in Taunton Deane held by the bishops of Winchester.

woodland cover and also, near Hayne, of a hedged enclosure for preserving game. A similar enclosure lay near Dipford in Trull, set once again in a wooded landscape. And for travelling over the Anglo-Saxon Vale, there were the roads, both major and minor, which the charters also record. Such routes included the surviving main road (the 'herepath') from Taunton to Wellington and the 'old street' (perhaps built by the Romans or known to them) leading north from Wiveliscombe through Ford to Elworthy.

But it is one remote landmark high in the Quantocks which evokes most powerfully the unknown people who filled the Anglo-Saxon landscape and shaped it to their needs. This 10th-century landmark, recorded at Merridge Hill on the far borders of Bishops Lydeard, was the *Motleah*, 'the place of assembly at the *leah*'. There, on a characteristically hilltop site, close to the round barrows sacred to the Bronze Age, the people of the district met to deliberate and to see justice done.

THE PIECEMEAL GRANTING of estates continued throughout the Anglo-Saxon centuries. But two transactions surpassed all others in their significance for the future. One took place at an unknown date in the first decade of the 10th century when King Edward the Elder granted to Asser, bishop of Sherborne, an estate comprising Wellington,

West Buckland and Bishops Lydeard. The new estate passed to the bishops of Wells following the creation of their new diocese in 909; but that was a minor disruption to an ecclesiastical lordship destined to endure till the 16th century.

Another yet grander transaction took place during 904, when Edward the Elder and Bishop Denewulf of Winchester met to confer at the royal hunting lodge at Bickleigh in Devon. It was there that the two men made a bargain of the greatest significance both for the See of Winchester and for the history of the Vale: the bishop and his successors, in return for lands in Somerset and beyond, were granted possession of the Taunton minster with all its widespread territories. Those territories would be added to for at least a century more, until the estate which became known as the manor of Taunton Deane was among the largest and most prosperous in all England. It reached from Ruishton in the east to a western outpost at Withiel Florey, and from Lydeard St Lawrence in the north to Otterford on Somerset's southern border. The intimate history of the area remains obstinately obscure throughout the 10th century, but the framework upon which the fabric of its later development would be woven was now complete. Taunton and its neighbours were Winchester land, and so they would remain, with hardly an interruption, for more than 900 years.

2

Distant Lords

WILLIAM OF WYKEHAM, bishop of Winchester, lies buried in his cathedral church beneath a splendid tomb. Jane Austen's simple grave slab, close at hand, is a reminder that not all greatness is given to display. But within the Gothic spaces of the cathedral, Wykeham and his fellow bishops inevitably dominate. The cathedral nave—one of the glories of the Middle Ages—was almost fin- ished when Wykeham died in 1404, and stands as the culmination to many centuries of build- ing and rebuilding on the site. It is, as well, a vivid expression of great wealth and power. 'Canterbury has the finer stable', one 14th- century bishop remarked, 'but Winchester has the deeper manger', a boast justified by the fact that in the whole Christian world only the archbishopric of Milan was worth more.

20 Effigy of William of Wykeham (1324–1404), bishop of Winchester and chancellor of England. The effigy marks Wykeham's burial place on the south side of the nave in Winchester Cathedral.

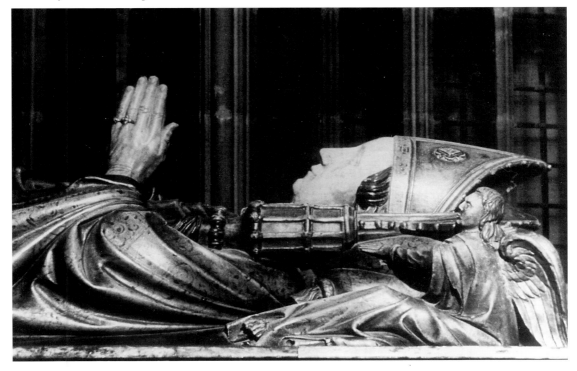

21 Pipe roll, or account roll, for the estates of the bishopric of Winchester, 1336-7. The roll opens with accounts for the Taunton estate.

The importance of the bishopric was established early as a result of Winchester's place at the heart of Anglo-Saxon Wessex, and the men appointed to serve as bishops during the Middle Ages were nearly always distinguished by their great ability and by the enjoyment of royal favour. They included no fewer than two cardinals, two Keepers of the Privy Seal, four Treasurers, and 10 Chancellors of England. The wealth of their bishopric was founded on the possession of vast landed estates, most of which, like Taunton itself, were acquired before the Norman Conquest. Though concentrated within Hampshire, those estates were scattered through seven southern counties, reaching east as far as Southwark on the banks of the Thames, and west as far as the Somerset outposts of Rimpton and Taunton. Not only was Taunton the most distant of all the estates from the central administration at Winchester. It was also the largest and most profitable, usually taking

pride of place at the head of the bishops' accounting records, the pipe rolls.

The bishops did not take control of their Taunton estate all at once. Their original purchase in 904 seems to have brought them no more than a title deed, and only later in the 10th century did King Edgar, with encouragement from Bishop Aethelwold, make Winchester's ownership a practical reality. He ordered his thegns at Taunton to hold their land in conformity with the bishop's wishes, or else to give it up. In addition, he gave almost princely powers to Aethelwold by granting him wide judicial privileges. Henceforth, the thegns and peasants of Taunton Deane would be as fully subject to the bishops of Winchester as those who lived on royal manors were to the king. When, in about 1044, Edward the Confessor (or perhaps his queen) added Pitminster to the estate, the local dominance of the bishops was finally complete.

THE ADVENT of Norman rule in 1066 began a period of rising prosperity both for the Winchester estate at Taunton and for the Vale as a whole. By the time Domesday Book was compiled in 1086, Taunton Deane was among the most densely-settled areas in the county, and contained some estates whose recorded value had more than doubled since the Conquest. Milverton, worth £12 in 1066, was valued at £25 in Domesday Book, and even tiny Heathfield had increased in value from 30s. to £4. But nowhere was change more apparent than on the Winchester lands. In the course of twenty years they had tripled in value to £170.

The estate which generated this vast amount was not only large but very complex. At its centre was Taunton whose urban status had become clear beyond doubt in the century before the Conquest. The town was already a marketing centre with some of the freedoms of a borough when Bishop Aelfheah died in 951; and at least from the reign of Aethelred the Unready (969-1014) it was also the site of a mint. Domesday records that the market and the mint each rendered 50s. a year, and the 64 burgesses the borough then possessed made Taunton one of the largest towns in Somerset after Bath, Ilchester and Milborne Port.

In the countryside which surrounded Taunton were the lands held by the bishop as his home farm, together with the holdings occupied by his tenants: these lands later included Bishops Hull, Wilton, Staplegrove, Kingston, Ruishton, Trull, Pitminster, Corfe, Stoke St Mary and Otterford, and became known as the 'infaring' of the manor of Taunton Deane. Other estates, mostly farther from the town, acknowledged the bishop as overlord and owed attendance at his courts in Taunton. But they functioned in most respects as independent manors and throughout the Middle Ages were governed by their own lords. These manors, nearly thirty in number, later made up the 'outfaring' or 'liberty' of the Taunton estate and included Oake, Cheddon Fitzpaine, Nynehead, Combe Florey, Lydeard St Lawrence, Hillfarrance, Norton Fitzwarren, Bradford on Tone, Heathfield, Halse, Bagborough and Orchard Portman.

22 & 23   Silver penny of Harold II, minted at Taunton by the moneyer Brihtric, 1066.

24 Effigies of Sir John de Meriet (d.1327) and his two wives Mary and Elizabeth in the north aisle of the church of SS Peter and Paul, Combe Florey. Sir John was lord of Combe Florey, part of the 'outfaring' of the Taunton estate, and acknowledged the bishop of Winchester as his overlord.

25 The Town Mill, Taunton, by Harry Frier, 1891. The Town Mill (or Town Mills) probably stood close to the site of one of the Domesday mills associated with Taunton. It was rebuilt in 1218-19 when the bishop's new fulling mill evidently displaced it, and was finally demolished in 1958. Its site was in the present Goodland Gardens, where the mill stream survives.

Domesday Book allows us to draw a few conclusions about the landscape occupied by these diverse communities. Woodland was plentiful and included 400 acres at Pitminster, the largest area recorded anywhere in Domesday Somerset. Cattle, pigs, sheep and goats were all present in moderate numbers to graze the abundant pasture. But arable farming was clearly predominant. The Winchester estate had arable land for as many as 120 ploughs; and to grind the corn such land produced there were at least three mills associated with Taunton and numerous others elsewhere, including two each at Norton Fitzwarren and Wellington.

THOUGH DOMESDAY BOOK is filled with detail about the Norman Vale, the information it provides is quite overshadowed by our far greater ignorance. Social arrangements, farming practices and settlement patterns are all largely unknown, and even the early Norman borough of Taunton has never been found archaeologically. The redevelopment of the town centre in 1996 did reveal rubbish pits of about the 11th century in the area of the Parade, suggesting some level of domestic occupation at that period. But structural evidence has never been found, and it seems quite probable that 11th-century Taunton was not focused on the modern town centre. One theory suggests that the Saxon town may eventually be discovered on rising ground to the west, close to County Hall.

It was in an extraordinary burst of activity during the century after Domesday Book that recognisable form was given to the town we have inherited. Evidence that Taunton was replanned during the 12th century is less conclusive than on other Winchester manors.

But it seems probable nonetheless that a decision taken in that period led to the refocusing of the town on a largely new site, perhaps following the fire which destroyed the place called 'Taintona' in 1111.

Major elements of Taunton's geography must already have been ancient. The route which enters from East Reach and leads west to Wellington and Exeter probably offered one pre-existing axis for development; so too

26 A late Saxon, probably 10th-century, circular brooch made of tin/lead alloy. The brooch was found in 1973 on the site in Corporation Street, Taunton, now occupied by Michael Paul House. The drawing shows the badly-damaged brooch as it would originally have appeared.

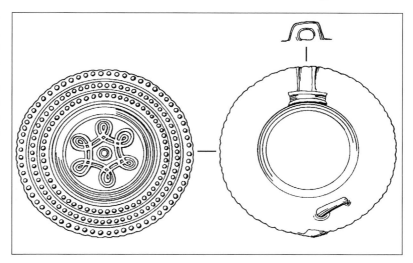

27 East Reach, Taunton, looking east, c.1910.

28 The medieval Tone Bridge, Taunton, *c.*1810, from a watercolour made in 1908 by Harry Frier after an earlier print. The bridge may have been built close to a ford by which the river was originally crossed and incorporated Sealy's Island, on which buildings stood. The bridge was rebuilt in 1810, 1834 and 1895.

may the route leading north across the river to Norton Fitzwarren and Kingston. Much else, however, was entirely new. Evidence recovered in 1996 suggests that the triangular site at the centre of the town had been laid out and pitched with cobbles by the early 12th century to provide a spacious market place (later known as the Island and the Cornhill). A defensive boundary bank and ditch—complete with north and east gates and probably a timber pallisade—surrounded the borough by 1158, and by the end of the century a formal arrangement of burgage plots had been created at least on the south side of Fore Street. But nothing more powerfully suggests the new beginning being made at Taunton in the 12th century than the building of a castle just outside the borough boundary.

The chosen site was in the area known as Castle Green, where the administrative headquarters of the bishopric estate, together with the minster and its cemetery, may already have long existed. William Gifford, bishop from 1107 to 1129, is usually credited with having begun the new work there, building a great hall supported on a stone-vaulted undercroft. A little later, the raising of a keep tower, in what is now the garden of the *Castle Hotel*, established beyond doubt the defensive nature of the site. The Annals of Winchester suggest that this massively strong tower was originally built in 1138 for the great Bishop Henry de Blois, the brother of King Stephen. It was destroyed in 1155 by order of Henry II, but was evidently soon rebuilt and was destined to remain a dominant feature of the Taunton skyline for the next 500 years.

29 Taunton Castle, *c.*1791, shortly after its restoration by Sir Benjamin Hammet. The bishop's chamber occupied the upper floor on the far left; his bedchamber may have been in the round tower; the chapel of St Nicholas was on the upper floor to the right of the round tower; and the exchequer chamber, where the manor records were kept, was above the late 15th-century gatehouse. The medieval chapel of St Peter, possibly successor to the Saxon minster, may have stood in the area in front of the castle.

30 Foundations of part of the castle keep, revealed during excavations in 1924-9. By the 14th century, the keep tower included five turrets, a hall, and a soldiers' chamber.

During the later 12th and the 13th centuries the complex of buildings and defences on the castle site reached its greatest extent. In 1208-9, Bishop Gifford's great hall and its associated buildings were surrounded by a curtain wall, and in the same period two moats were dug to define the inner and outer baileys (or wards) of the castle. Further intense activity followed in the years 1245-9, when William Raleigh was bishop of Winchester. Superintended by Master John the Carpenter and Master Walter the Mason, an army of workmen remodelled the great hall in its present form as a ground-floor room, rebuilt the bishop's chamber (now the Somerset Room), and provided the castle with its own chapel of St Nicholas. Stone was brought from Ham Hill along the rivers Parrett and Tone to a landing-place at Ruishton, and other stone came from quarries at Hestercombe. Large sums were spent on the necessary lead and iron work for the new buildings, and the accounts record as well the money paid for 32,000 lath nails, 16,000 tile nails, 6,800 board nails and 5,500 floor nails. The constable of the castle, the bishop's principal officer at Taunton, had his own hall which probably adjoined the castle east gate (Castle Bow), and other buildings on the same site accommodated the janitor, the watchmen and the clerk.

The rapid growth of the castle from the 12th century onwards must soon have affected its likely neighbour, the minster church. William Gifford, despite strong opposition, converted the minster into a priory of Augustinian canons in about 1120, and in 1158 any competing demands for space at Castle Green were finally resolved by Henry de Blois. He provided a new site for the priory among fields and meadows outside the borough's north-eastern boundary. There, in the setting of the priory complex, the monastic community was destined to remain until the Dissolution in 1539.

THE DEVELOPMENT of the priory and castle sites in the 12th and 13th centuries was matched by the continuing growth of Taunton itself. In the first half of the 13th century suburban expansion was taking place in the East Reach area beyond the borough's east gate, as well as on the north side of the river at Mill Lane (North Town) and at Shuttern. It occurred more strikingly at Canon Street, Middle Street and St James's Street. These three streets, dating at least from the 13th century, were evidently a planned extension to the town and rose on land owned by Taunton Priory.

Taunton's role as a centre of trade was also developing rapidly. It attracted custom from afar not only to its market, but also to its two annual fairs: the first of these, the borough fair, was held around St Botolph's day, 17 June; the second, granted by Henry III in 1256, took place at Mill Lane around 7 July, feast of the translation of St Thomas Becket. That Taunton people, in their turn, became increasingly familiar with distant markets is suggested by the charter which, in about 1136, King Stephen issued to the borough. To 'the burgesses of Taunton, the men of the bishop of Winchester' he granted the same freedom from tolls and passage dues as was enjoyed throughout the land by citizens of London and Winchester. Even Bristol waited almost twenty more years before acquiring such privileges, and Taunton's good fortune may indicate once again the influence of Henry de Blois.

From at least 1266, stalls were becoming permanent structures in the market place, while the High Street, first mentioned in the 14th century, was probably created in the same period to provide additional space on market days. By 1321 a market cross had been built near the junction of Fore Street and High Street, and elsewhere around the market place the Chuse (?Cheese) Cross and the Rix or Ruish Cross are later recorded. The Guildhall, raised on pillars, was built on the western side

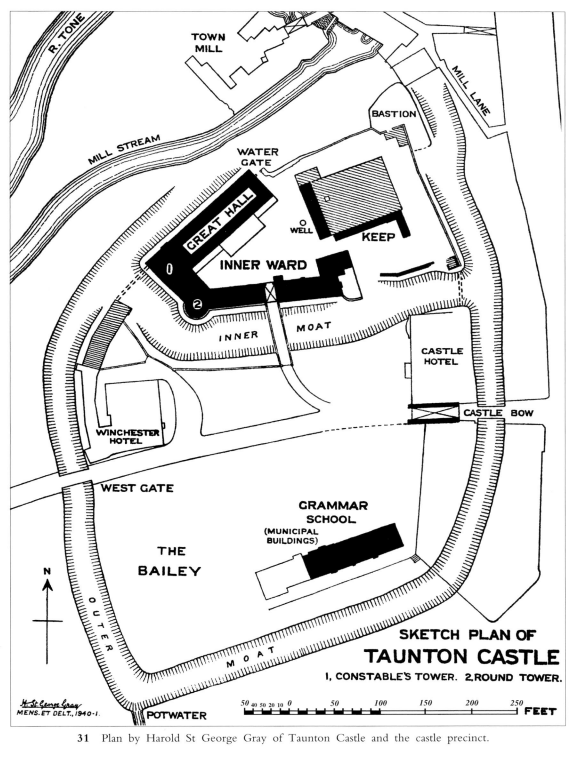

31 Plan by Harold St George Gray of Taunton Castle and the castle precinct.

32 *Above*. High Street, Taunton, looking north towards the town centre, *c*.1865. High Street may have been a 13th-century addition to the town plan.

33 *Below left*. The west wall of Taunton's 15th-century Guildhall, revealed in February 1996 during the town centre redevelopment. The building survived until 1770. (*See also* illustration 75.)

34 *Below right*. Taunton's High Cross or Market Cross which stood near the junction of Fore Street and High Street. The structure as illustrated here appears to have been late medieval. It was finally demolished, with the consent of the bishop of Winchester, in 1771.

of the island site in 1467, close to the ancient conduit which provided the market with water. On the eastern side, the process of encroachment, which by the 17th century had filled half the market place with inns and other buildings, was already under way during the Middle Ages.

The tradesmen of late 13th-century Taunton included butchers, bakers, fishmongers, cutlers, glovers, shoemakers, smiths and wine merchants. But none were more important to the prosperity of the medieval town than the cloth merchants and textile workers whose names and activities are recorded with increasing frequency. The making of cloth must certainly have been a domestic occupation in the Vale from early times. Not until the 13th century, however, did Taunton take a larger part in what soon became one of England's most significant trades. The Winchester pipe roll for 1218-9 details the work of masons and carpenters who built a water-powered fulling mill at Taunton

that year. This pioneering mill, which stood on the banks of the Tone near Taunton Castle, was used for washing and thickening newly-woven cloth, and is almost the earliest such mill recorded in the West Country. More were to follow, including the 'new fulling mill' mentioned at Bishops Hull in 1246.

For the remainder of the Middle Ages, many of the town's leading citizens were closely connected with the cloth trade. Robert Aysell, an MP for Taunton in 1397, was taxed on no fewer than 283 'dozens' of cloth which he sold in Somerset during 1395-7. John Marchaunt, who represented Taunton in 12 Parliaments, sold 69 'dozens' in the same period, as well as importing madder for use in cloth finishing. It was little wonder that, when in the 14th century the customs by which the borough was governed were set down in writing, rules to protect the town's cloth trade took pride of place.

35   Fore Street, Taunton, by J.C. Buckler, 1832. The building in the centre, now called the *Tudor Tavern*, is of 14th-century origin and until the early 15th century was owned by the Marchaunt family. It was then acquired by the Portmans whose tenant, Thomas Trowbridge, evidently added the timber-framed façade in 1578. The Portmans later reserved the right to use the building's 'great chamber' when Assizes or Quarter Sessions were sitting at Taunton.

THE WOOL which sustained this burgeoning industry, and the other agricultural produce which supplied the town's markets and fairs, came not least from the bishop's 'infaring' lands within the Vale. The area was far too large to manage as one unit, and by the later 13th century had been organised into the five infaring 'hundreds' of Holway, Hull, Poundisford, Staplegrove and Nailsbourne. These hundreds in their turn contained dozens of manorial 'tithings', some of them bearing familiar names such as Ruishton, Stoke, Obridge and Rumwell. And overseeing the whole complex structure on the bishop's behalf was an array of manorial officials—chiefly drawn from the ranks of the tenantry—who included reeves, bedells, haywards and woodwards, together with more obscure officials such as the keepers of the waterlete. There were also many permanent estate labourers.

36 A deer depicted on a 16th-century bench end at St Mary's Church, Bishops Lydeard.

The territory in their care was extensive. The infaring as a whole contained more than 11,000 acres of agricultural land, of which some 3,000 acres, dispersed through the five hundreds, were managed for the bishop as his home farm or demesne. The best of the demesne land was in the hundreds of Holway, Hull and Staplegrove, and was chiefly used in the production of grain. Less fertile soils were better suited to pastoral farming, and Nailsbourne hundred accordingly became home for much of the estate's sheep flock, Poundisford for its pig and dairy herds. In each of the hundreds the farming of the demesne was directed from a central barton generally located in the place from which the hundred took its name: a barton farm existed, for example, near each of the hamlets of Holway, Poundisford and Nailsbourne. Why these places, minor even in the Middle Ages, were chosen to fulfil such important functions is not immediately clear, though all of them are strongly associated with known or suspected Roman occupation. It is not impossible, therefore, that the bartons were direct successors to Romano-British farms or villas from which, one thousand years before, the agriculture of some part of the Roman Vale had been controlled.

The impact of the bishops on the rural landscape was not confined to their activities as arable and pastoral farmers. Their woodlands—greatly prized and carefully protected—dominated sites at 'Knoll' on Stoke Hill, Hamwood in Trull, 'Haidwood' at Haydon, Pickeridge in Corfe and Bishopswood in Otterford. Their parks and fishponds, both in the Vale and throughout the bishopric estates, left a yet more conspicuous mark and were the certain proof of great status. Poundisford Park, like many of the bishopric parks, was probably a 12th-century creation, and in 1210 was extended by more than 100 acres. There the episcopal deer were protected, both as a source of venison for the bishop's table and to provide hunting for the bishop and his guests on infrequent journeys into Somerset. The park at

37 Vivary Park, Taunton, *c.*1910. The park was created in its present form in 1896 and occupies the site of the medieval fishponds, or *vivaria*, of the bishops of Winchester. In the foreground is the artificial channel dug in 1332 to carry water from Sherford stream to the town.

Nailsbourne, created soon after 1232, was more exotically stocked with cranes, peacocks, and a flock of troublesome swans, and like Poundisford was also used for breeding horses. A third park at Pickeridge, the 'new park', followed in mid-century, close to the park above Hayne created by the prior of Taunton. The bishopric fishponds, or *vivaria*, were probably further creations of the extraordinary 12th century and lay in the area of Vivary Park. The two ponds may have covered at least 100 acres, and supplied pike, bream, perch and eels for use in Lent as well as on fish days throughout the year. When Henry III and his retinue passed through Taunton in 1220-1, they consumed 24 sticks of the bishop's eels (at 15 eels to the stick); 10 years later the vast sum of £8 3s. 9d. was paid to carry live bream from Taunton to Winchester on a journey which lasted 15 days.

The vast demesne could never have been farmed without the labour services of a feudal tenantry. William de Mora, a tenant at Holway in the mid-13th century, was one of many who were obliged to plough an acre for the lord in winter and another in Lent, as well as to sow, harrow and weed the land. William did additional ploughing as 'boonwork', and in the great communal effort of the summer and autumn helped to gather in the lord's harvest. At Christmas, he brought firewood to the castle if the bishop was staying there and, when the bishop set out from Taunton, William and his fellows carried the lord's belongings as far as Rimpton. Other tenants, especially those living on the eastern fringes of the manor, acted as messengers, or would drive cattle to other markets. And, as a constant reminder of unfree status, no tenant could live outside the manor, or arrange for his daughter's marriage, without

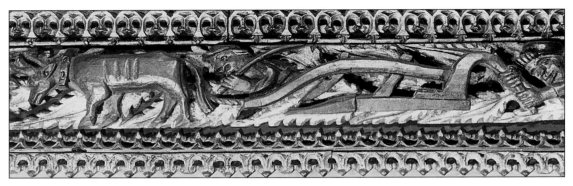

38 Ploughing with oxen depicted on the chancel screen at All Saints' Church, Norton Fitzwarren, *c.*1500.

39 Bradford on Tone, *c.*1840.

first making payment to the bishop. Nor could a tenant grind his corn anywhere but in the lord's mills, of which there were 12 on the Taunton estate by the 13th century.

Just as the bishop needed his tenants to farm the demesne, so too they depended on him to provide economic and physical protection and to supply them with the land they farmed for themselves. Tenant lands in the infaring hundreds lay side by side with those of the bishop, and included holdings which ranged in size from the plots of the almost landless to farms of thirty or forty acres. Some land was probably farmed in enclosures, as is the case today. But other extensive areas lay in large, strip-cultivated, open fields, whose fossilised traces can still be seen throughout the district and especially in places such as

Stoke St Mary and Ruishton. The creation of these communal fields was probably one aspect of major settlement changes which seem to have been complete by the 12th century. Amidst the ancient pattern of small farms and hamlets, larger 'nucleated' villages began to appear, some of them, like Ruishton or the outfaring village of Bradford, planned as a clear network of streets. With their open fields around them, these enlarged and at least partly replanned settlements emphasised co-operative patterns of living and farming, and have survived for us as the villages of the modern Vale. Their creation, which was paralleled at various dates in many parts of England, achieved a transformation of the landscape no less profound than that which affected the 12th-century borough of Taunton.

THE POPULATION of the estate rose steadily during the 13th and early 14th centuries, and the pressures on available land may often have been acute. Some tenants added to their land by reclaiming areas of waste and scrub, especially on the hills at Corfe, Pitminster and Otterford; some evidently sought work in the borough, settling just outside the borough boundaries in new squatter-like communities; and some, especially young males, left the estate altogether in search of land or employment. In 1315-16, the failure of the harvest marked the beginning of crisis years which reached their terrible culmination with the first visitation of the Black Death in 1348-9. At least half the local population may have perished in this calamity. By the autumn of 1349 more than fifty holdings in Poundisford hundred lay empty because their tenants were dead, and by 1351 there were still more than 200 vacant holdings over the estate as a whole. The Bishop of Bath and Wells found safety at his country seat in Wiveliscombe while the threat of infection lasted; but the 'pestilence' was in general no respecter of persons. Amongst the hundreds throughout the Vale who fell victim were evidently two successive vicars of Pitminster and Walter Foxcote, Taunton's priest.

Though land in the Vale did not remain unoccupied for long, the Black Death, and the second pestilence of 1361-2, hastened the decline of old patterns of agriculture. Wage labour grew in importance and areas of demesne were more regularly leased to enterprising tenants. The impatience of Taunton people with old obligations found violent expression in 1410. Four hundred townsmen took to the streets, assaulted the bishop's officers collecting tolls for the fair, and vowed to 'live and die' against their overlord. The great Cardinal Beaufort, then bishop of Winchester, became the last of the medieval bishops to visit Taunton when, shortly afterwards, he arrived at the castle

40 Cardinal Henry Beaufort (d.1447), bishop of Winchester, the last of the medieval bishops to visit Taunton.

with a retine of several hundred. A total of 579 men laboured to overhaul the building before his arrival and, when he left, a further 379 men carried out the works he had ordered. But these massive building works were almost the last great expression of episcopal power. In 1418, Beaufort acknowledged the reality of change by giving up demesne farming at Taunton altogether, and in the years that followed hundreds of acres of demesne land were let to tenants.

BEAUFORT'S SUDDEN RETREAT from Taunton, though typical of developments throughout the bishopric estates at that period, marked an important loosening of ties between Taunton and its ancient masters. The bishops' locally-elected officials, including the two borough portreeves and their assistants the bailiffs and the constables, continued to regulate many aspects of life through an elaborate system of courts. But it is likely nonetheless that the increasing remoteness of the bishops, and the absence of a powerful gentry, encouraged intolerance of authority and independence of spirit among local people, characteristics for which they later became notorious.

Already traders and merchants within the borough had taken important powers into their own hands by creating the merchant guild of St Martin, first recorded in the borough customs of the 14th century; the same document refers also to 'the panel of the borough', presumably an early decision-making body; and from 1290 onwards Taunton had been sending two representatives to Parliament, often selecting them from the ranks of its wealthiest merchants.

The town's readiness to assert its independence from authority was powerfully expressed in the support it gave to Perkin Warbeck, pretender to the throne of Henry VII. Warbeck claimed to be Edward IV's second son, one of the Princes in the Tower, and growing numbers, including the King of Scotland himself, found it convenient to believe him. When, early in 1497, taxes were imposed

to finance an English campaign against the Scots, the people of Cornwall rose in protest and marched on London several thousand strong. The provost of Penrhyn, one of the hated tax collectors, fled eastwards before them. But near Taunton he was captured by a body of Cornish rebels who brought him in triumph to the town 'and there in the market place slewe hym pytuously, in such wise that he was dismembred and kutte in many and sundry peces'.

Though the Cornish rising ended in defeat at Blackheath on 17 June, it was Cornwall that Warbeck now chose as the starting-point for his most concerted attempt to depose King Henry. He arrived from Ireland near Land's End on 7 September 1497, was proclaimed King Richard IV at Bodmin, then marched towards Exeter with an army of some 3,000 Cornishmen. He failed to take the heavily-defended city from the Earl of Devon, and when, on 20 September, his forces, now some 8,000 strong, mustered in fields outside Taunton, he was demoralised and fearful. At midnight he fled secretly, leaving his supporters to their fate, but on 5 October was brought back as a prisoner to Taunton to face Henry VII for the first time.

At their meeting, which probably took place in Taunton Castle, the king, surrounded by his nobles, addressed the imposter:

> We have heard that you call yourself Richard, son of King Edward. In this place are some who were companions of that lord. Look and see if you recognise them.

But Warbeck replied that he did not know any of them and at once confessed his true identity to be Piers Osbeck, son of a prosperous citizen of Tournai in Flanders. The king, to the consternation of many, at first spared Warbeck's life—he was not executed until 1499—and his supporters in the West suffered only in their pockets. At Taunton a total of £1,298 10s. was levied in fines on inhabitants of the manor and the borough, a vast sum evidently reflecting the enthusiasm with which Warbeck's cause had been embraced. One Taunton merchant, John Toose, was fined no less than £100.

The defeat of Warbeck's rebellion was decisive for the king, marking the moment when he could begin to hope that the dynastic struggles of the 15th century were finally at an end. Taunton was lucky to escape so lightly from the consequences of disloyalty, and indeed there is some reason to suppose that it was soon reconciled with the powers it had defied. Richard Fox, bishop of Winchester from 1501 to 1528, and for long one of Henry VII's most trusted advisers, built a grammar school at Taunton in 1521-2. It survives today as the Municipal Buildings, and offers a reminder not only of the turmoils which brought the Middle Ages to a close, but of the long relationship, so often fruitful, between Taunton and its lords.

41 Richard Fox (?1448-1528), bishop of Winchester.

42 Taunton Grammar School, by Harry Frier, 1912, after an earlier print. The school was built by Bishop Fox in 1521-2 and may have been the successor to an existing foundation. A school existed at Taunton as early as 1286.

3

The Age of Faith

THE MEN AND WOMEN of the medieval Vale inhabited a world ruled not only by economic and political forces, but also by the power of the Christian Church. No life was untouched by religion, and the images of doom and salvation, so often depicted in medieval churches, stood for a reality no less compelling than a busy market day on Taunton Cornhill.

43 The Resurrection, depicted by Simon Warman on a 16th-century bench end in the church of St John the Baptist, Hatch Beauchamp. Christ climbs from an altar-like tomb while the guards recoil in fear.

The creation of the Vale's churches and parishes was a complex process which seems to have been completed near the end of the 12th century. The ancient mother church at Taunton, founded by the West Saxon royal house over four centuries earlier, was probably central to that process. Its earliest Anglo-Saxon clergy may have evangelised a large part of Taunton Deane, encouraging the creation of daughter churches both in the immediate area of the town and possibly at a greater distance as well. By the time of the Norman Conquest, however, the royal estate in the Vale had long since been broken up, the minster had been acquired by the bishop of Winchester, and its only remaining daughter churches lay scattered within the boundaries of the bishop's great Taunton estate.

During the 12th century, when the minster at Taunton was reformed as an Augustinian priory, surviving documents at last add detail to the picture. They record that in 1162 the churches, or chapels, which belonged to the priory included the chief town church of St Mary Magdalene, its near neighbour the church of St James, and at least eleven other churches in the parishes around. The priory derived a substantial income from these parishes by way of tithes and other dues, and claimed the people of at least some of them for burial after death. It was the existence of such burial customs which helped to fill the early minster cemetery, probably located on Castle Green, as well as its replacement, the priory's lay cemetery, recently discovered near Canon

Street. The parish of St Mary Magdalene gained the right to bury its own dead only in 1446—though there is almost no evidence that the right was exercised before the Reformation—and 30 years later the parish of Trull successfully petitioned for the same privilege. But until the Dissolution in 1539 the dead of Orchard Portman, Ruishton, Staplegrove and Stoke St Mary continued to be brought over difficult roads for burial at Taunton Priory.

The canons of the priory may at first have continued to serve the daughter churches as the minster priests had done before them. But the demands of their communal life were too often distracting, and villagers sometimes died before receiving the last rites because no priest could be found in time. Finally, in 1308, an agreement was reached which transferred some of the pastoral burden to the recently-created vicar of St Mary's Church. The vicar, in return for an allowance of bread and ale, feed for his horse and an annual salary of £10, took responsibility for St Mary's Church, the castle chapels of St Nicholas and St Peter, and the

44 *Top*. St John's Church, Staplegrove, by Harry Frier, 1892. The church, whose earliest elements appear to be of the 13th century, was one of the daughter churches of Taunton Priory.

45 *Above*. Leaden seal, or *bulla*, of Pope Sixtus IV (reigned 1471-84), found in the River Tone near the site of Taunton Priory. The archives of the priory (of which almost none survive) may have been thrown into the river or otherwise destroyed soon after the Dissolution.

churches of Trull and Wilton. At the same time, the prior agreed to find a priest to be shared by St James's Church and Staplegrove, and another to serve at Ruishton and Stoke St Mary. Not even these new arrangements were always successful. In 1353, the priest who served at St James's and Staplegrove complained bitterly that the prior had denied him his stipend as well as the bread and beer that he was due; and in 1415 the Pope himself instructed the prior to make sure that mass was duly celebrated in the priory's daughter churches.

TAUNTON PRIORY SURVIVED for more than 400 years, and throughout the later Middle Ages dominated the religious life of the area. The priory was dedicated to St Peter and St Paul, like the cathedral church in Winchester, and owed its creation and early development to the patronage of the bishops of Winchester. It was founded as an Augustinian house in about 1120. But the growth of its local power and prestige evidently dated from 1158, when Bishop Henry de Blois gave the priory its new site

46 St Margaret's Hospital, by L.C. Hammett, 1921. The 'house of lepers of St Margaret' was probably founded during the 12th century by the prior of Taunton and stood on the edge of the town in West Monkton parish. The hospital was evidently rebuilt by Richard Bere (d.1524), abbot of Glastonbury and lord of West Monkton, and later served as an almshouse until 1936. Its associated chapel belonged to Taunton Priory but did not survive the Reformation.

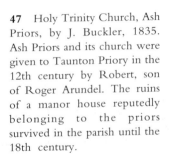

47 Holy Trinity Church, Ash Priors, by J. Buckler, 1835. Ash Priors and its church were given to Taunton Priory in the 12th century by Robert, son of Roger Arundel. The ruins of a manor house reputedly belonging to the priors survived in the parish until the 18th century.

48 St James's Street, Taunton, by J.C. Buckler, 1832. St James's Church, on the right, was first recorded in the 12th century and served a suburb of the town which developed on priory land outside the borough boundary. On the left are late 15th-century almshouses, demolished in 1897, which were probably founded by the priory.

just outside the borough boundary. Bishop Henry provided not just the land, close to the present St James's Church, where the priory complex was created during the next two centuries. His gift included a much wider area bounded on the north by the River Tone, on the south and west by East Reach and the borough boundary and on the east by the Abbot of Glastonbury's manor of West Monkton. An extensive 'moor' on the opposite bank of the Tone, acquired earlier in the century, contained the area later known as Prior's Wood; and at Pitminster the prior and canons held not only the Church of St Andrew and its chapelry at Otterford, but extensive lands which later contained a deer park, fishponds and a grange farm (Barton Grange). Other gifts brought them churches

and lands in such places as Ash Priors, Tolland, Thurloxton, Dulverton, Wilton, Thurlbear and Nynehead, and ensured that the priory was important both as a spiritual focus and as the centre of a large estate.

Despite the extent of its landed wealth, Taunton Priory, like most Augustinian foundations, was a religious house of no more than middle rank. It could never compete in size or influence with the great Benedictine abbey at Glastonbury, and was far too poor to create a monastic house on the Glastonbury scale. The priory's living accommodation may have been built first, and not until 1277 is there any mention of the monastic church itself. In that year the church was beginning to rise 'in a style of costly magnificence', and the closing phases of construction were probably reached half a

49 The so-called Priory Barn in about 1865. The building, which evidently flanked a gateway, probably dates from the late 15th or early 16th centuries, and may originally have accommodated guests or lay members of the priory. Its two late 13th-century windows were probably salvaged from the priory at the Dissolution.

50 A canon regular of the order of St Augustine, after an engraving by Wenceslaus Hollar.

century later when, in the period 1327-37, the canons received permission to collect alms for finishing the work. Though so little evidence of the priory has survived, documents record a church which at its greatest extent included nave and choir, chapels of the Virgin and St Anthony, the greater altar, the high cross near the pulpit, the Trinity door, and the door and aisle of St Botolph. The cloister and the chapter house are also mentioned, as is the prior's house. The dormitory, refectory, infirmary and kitchen were further elements in the priory complex; and standing near the western boundaries of the site was the building now known as the Priory Barn, possibly in origin a structure flanking a gateway.

Like all religious houses, Taunton Priory was founded to offer worship to God. But the pastoral responsibilities inherited from the past also created an enduring bond with the world outside, and ensured that the priory canons, dressed in the black hooded robes of their order, were a familiar sight in the streets of Taunton. Twenty-six canons were recorded in 1339, 15 in 1377 and 1476, and only 12 when the deed of surrender was signed in 1539. Many of them, including a 14th-century sub-prior, John Russchton (or Ruishton), were probably local men. Others such as Robert of Alresford or Thomas Ufculme were evidently recruits from afar. The religious calling which brought such men to the priory was not always proof against their human frailty. In 1353, the alleged misdeeds of one of the canons, Robert Cundyt, included wandering after curfew, embezzling money and goods, 'incontinence with a certain woman', and threatening to break the prior's head. When Bishop Beckington made his visitation in 1451 he clearly found much that troubled him. He ordered that in future the canons were to be in their dormitory by eight at night, that they were not to invite women to their chambers or to eat and drink with them there, that any who swore by the limbs of God were to fast on bread and water, and that due reverence was to be shown at all times by lesser canons to their seniors.

Though the priors themselves did not always escape criticism, some at least were clearly distinguished men. The first prior, Guy of Merton, enjoyed a high reputation for his scholarship, despite antagonising the canons by his obsessive devotion to the poor; Thomas Benet, a 15th-century prior, was amongst those summoned to attend the Council of Ferrara in 1438; and in 1499 Prior John Prowse was granted special privileges by the Pope including the right to use a pastoral staff and other regalia of a bishop.

The elaborate procedures by which new priors were elected are described in a number of records surviving from the 14th century onwards. Soon after Prior Ralph de Colmpstoke resigned his office in 1339, the canons gathered in the chapter house and chose their fellow canon, Robert de Messyngham, to be Prior Ralph's successor. Together with their new prior they later walked in procession to the high altar and publicly announced the decision they had reached. On the election of Thomas Ufculme in 1413, a 'great crowd of clergy and people' gathered in the church to hear the news proclaimed; and in 1523, when William Yorke was chosen as prior, 'a solemn *Te Deum* accompanied by the organs' preceded the announcement, and the bells of the priory rang out across the Vale.

TAUNTON PRIORY OCCUPIED an important place in the lives of local people, but they reserved a yet greater devotion for their own parish churches. Much that now survives of those buildings is late medieval, though the evidence from Wilton, already noted, suggests that at least some local churches were being built in stone before the end of the Anglo-Saxon period. It was in the century after the Conquest, however, that there is strong evidence for major building campaigns. Of all the churches which must once have existed in the 12th-century Vale, the outstanding local survival is the early Norman church of St Thomas, Thurlbear, an aisled structure of

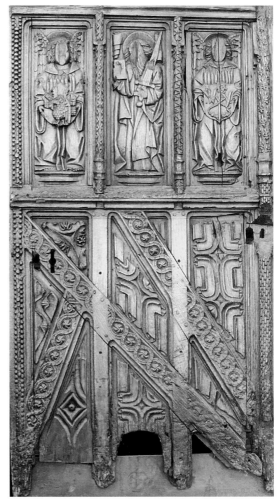

51 One of a pair of oak doors probably made for Taunton Priory, *c*.1525. The upper left panel contains the arms of Richard Fox, bishop of Winchester from 1501 to 1528, and the upper right panel the initials of William Yorke, nominated prior of Taunton in 1523.

eloquent simplicity which may have been built by Thurlbear's Domesday overlord, the Count of Mortain. Norman fonts such as those at Milverton, Angersleigh and Corfe remain from 12th-century churches which have otherwise largely vanished, and Norman doorways at Ruishton, Staple Fitzpaine and, especially, Orchard Portman, are further evidence for ambitious Norman churches. The church which

52 *Above left.* The Norman font, St Nicholas's Church, Corfe, by S.G. Tovey, 1846. The church was 'ruthlessly' restored in 1842 and 1858.

53 *Above right.* The late Norman north doorway at St Michael's Church, Orchard Portman, by George French, 1993. The doorway dates from the second half of the 12th century and is the most artistically ambitious Norman survival in Taunton Deane.

Wellington must certainly have possessed in that period may be represented by the wall footings recently discovered in the nave, and Victorian excavations in St Mary's Church, Taunton, also found possible traces of a Norman predecessor.

That so little now remains to commemorate the church builders of the Norman era reflects the piety and wealth of later generations and their determination to make room for yet more ambitious projects. Major work of the 13th and early 14th centuries survives at St Mary's in Taunton, as well as at Bishops Hull, Trull, Kingston, Bradford on Tone and West Buckland. But it was in the two centuries following the Black Death in 1348-9 that the transformation of the Vale's churches largely took place. New aisles, windows, doors and porches, built in the Perpendicular style of the late Middle Ages, appeared in churches throughout the district; benches were supplied for the benefit of congregations now increasingly used to hearing sermons preached; and elaborate timber screens and roodlofts were installed. The interior of St Mary's in Taunton shows what could be achieved by one of the wealthiest parishes in the West of England. Double aisles, almost unprecedented in a parish church, expressed grand architectural aspirations, and a splendid tie-beam roof, embellished with angels, covered the nave.

It is the smaller church interiors, however, and especially those containing original woodwork, which often have more power to move us. The little church at Broomfield, high on the Quantocks overlooking the Vale, contains 16th-century benches by the prolific Bicknoller craftsman, Simon Warman, together with an aisle for which money was left in 1535. Filled with light through the aisle's large north windows, the interior achieves a lucid stillness which is deeply memorable. Outstanding woodwork is also preserved at Bishops Lydeard, Kingston St Mary, Norton Fitzwarren and Hatch Beauchamp. But in no local church, and in few elsewhere, is the woodcarver's craft more impressively displayed than at Trull. An array of benches, many by Warman, crowd the nave, complementing a chancel screen

which retains some of its original colour and a timber pulpit which is among the most splendid in the West Country. Trull is also rare in preserving large amounts of 15th-century glass. It includes images of dragon-slaying saints and the delicately-drawn figure of the Virgin Mary shown in the east window weeping at the cross. But even Trull, like nearly all other local churches, contains no sign of the medieval wall paintings which must once have been so prominent.

However beautiful individual church interiors may be, Taunton Deane earns its special place in the history of architecture for the sake of some splendidly elaborate west towers. At Bishops Lydeard, Kingston St Mary, Staple Fitzpaine, Ruishton and Taunton's two parish churches new towers were built in about

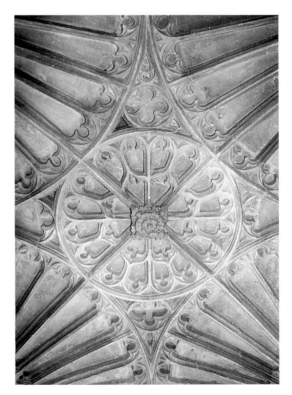

54 *Above left*. Part of the south nave arcade of St Giles's Church, Bradford on Tone. The simple cylindrical piers and double-chamfered arches date from about 1300.

55 *Above right*. Fan vault inside the early 16th-century south porch of St Mary's Church, Kingston St Mary.

56 *Above left.* Interior of the Church of St Mary Magdalene, Taunton, *c.*1880. The church is seen as it appeared after a series of controversial Victorian restorations.

57 *Above.* All Saints' Church, Broomfield, showing benches by Simon Warman, and the early 16th-century north aisle and arcade.

58 *Left.* Wooden pulpit in All Saints' Church, Trull, *c.*1500. The pulpit incorporates figures of St John the Evangelist, St Gregory, St Augustine of Hippo, St Jerome and St Ambrose. The figures are remarkable not only in themselves but because they survived the Reformation undefaced.

59 View of Bishops Lydeard by Miss Sweeting, *c.*1840.

60 St Mary's Church, Kingston St Mary, by J. Buckler, 1839. In 1950 Kenneth Wickham wrote: 'There is a mastery and beauty of design in the towers of Isle Abbots, Staple Fitzpaine, and Kingston which renders them among the greatest masterpieces of English architecture.'

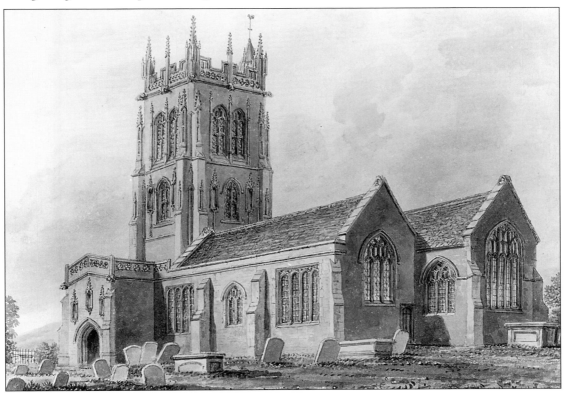

61 *Above left.* The tower of St Mary's, Taunton, the grandest and greatest of English church towers, seen from Hammet Street, *c.*1880. The tower was rebuilt as an exact copy of the original between 1858 and 1862.

62 *Above right.* Brass supposed to represent Henry Abyndon, rector of West Monkton, 1436-57.

the period 1450 to 1540, and are conspicuous proofs of the great wealth generated by the cloth trade. The towers at Bishops Lydeard and St James's, Taunton, may have been built first. They were followed before 1490 by those at Staple Fitzpaine and Kingston, and by the almost identical tower at Isle Abbots. These three related towers have been praised as perhaps the most artistically perfect of all the many towers built in medieval Somerset, combining beauty of form with richly-detailed pinnacles and parapets, window openings filled with tracery panels, and an abundance of grotesques and angel busts.

In grandeur of conception, however, nothing in the Vale remotely equals the great west tower of St Mary's Church in Taunton. Bequests to the building fund refer to the new tower from 1488 to 1499, to the pinnacles in 1502, to the finishing of the tower in 1504-5, and to the insertion of tracery panels for the windows in 1514. The completed tower, perhaps the greatest of all the parish church towers of England, was prodigious in its scale and ambition. Although it inevitably lacks the intimate beauty of smaller towers such as Kingston, Staple or Bishops Lydeard, it remains a triumphant expression of civic pride, merchant wealth and religious belief, and an artistic achievement to rank with the finest of the English Middle Ages.

THE PRIESTS WHO SERVED the churches of the Vale, like the canons of Taunton Priory, were in many cases born into local families. On a day at Wiveliscombe in 1315, John of Drokensford, bishop of Bath and Wells, ordained Richard Attewych of Fitzhead, Martin of Sandhill and John of Bicknoller into minor orders, and other 14th-century clergy whose names record their local origins included Robert of Tolland and Emeric of Orchard. Whether such men served faithfully and well is largely unknown to us, since only in cases where discipline broke down is a detailed record likely to survive. Thus, when in 1318 George Roges, rector of Staple Fitzpaine, admitted adultery, his crime was duly noted in the bishop's register, together with the fine of five marks that he paid. In 1419, the chaplain of Bishops Hull, Thomas Nicholas, suffered a far greater penalty for having taken a dispute over tithes to the secular authorities. Bishop Bubwith, evidently enraged, pronounced excommunication, and ordered that in penance Nicholas should be whipped through the church of Bishops Hull as well as through Taunton market place, on each occasion holding in his hand a candle weighing half a pound. Excommunication was also the fate in 1338 of Richard de Rokebere, vicar of Kingston St Mary. Quite how he had displeased the bishop is not certain, though Rokebere's defiance of him is vividly recorded. When the dean of Wells announced the excommunication to a congregation of over 200 in Kingston church, Rokebere merely replied, 'If the bishop has excommunicated me, I excommunicate him'. Then, putting on his vestments, he proceeded to celebrate mass while the congregation kept the dean a prisoner till service was over.

More often, the priests of the medieval Vale are recorded only on their appointment to serve in a church or chapel, or when they sought leave of absence, sometimes to study or to go on pilgrimage. In February 1320, William de Bath, rector of Bagborough, was given leave to visit the shrine at Santiago de Compostela, on condition that he returned to his parish by mid-summer. Three years later, Simon de Lym, vicar of St Mary's, set out for 'foreign shrines' as well as to visit the papal court in Rome. Many others had more worldly reasons to absent themselves, including Thomas Bal, rector of Oake. In 1354 he asked permission to remain in the service of Lady Margaret Beauchamp, evidently preferring to stay in her great house at Merryfield than to survive in ill-paid rural obscurity.

Of the great numbers of local clergy, only a minority enjoyed the relatively high status of a rector or vicar. Many others were no more than impoverished chantry priests or parochial chaplains who have left almost no trace. Chantry priests, in particular, were common in churches throughout the Vale and were employed to say masses for the souls of the departed, either by a particular benefactor or through the fundraising efforts of a parish guild. Sometimes, as at Milverton and Bradford, a separate chantry chapel was built next to the parish church. Usually, however, such priests presided at secondary altars or, as at Combe Florey, were based in a particular part of the church building, often the north aisle. So numerous did chantries become, especially in larger West Country churches, that by 1450 St Mary's, Taunton, was staffed by at least twelve priests. They were responsible for chantries which included those dedicated to the Virgin, St Anne and St Andrew, and helped to maintain the cycle of worship which filled the church each day. In 1444, the mass of the Virgin Mary, with plainsong, was celebrated at five or six in the morning, and was followed by a succession of further masses. Lauds, Matins and other offices were also said daily, and on Sundays and festivals high mass formed a centre-piece to the week's worship. Processions for Palm Sunday and other high days were part of church life at St Mary's by the beginning of the 16th century, as was the performance at Easter of 'Mary Magdaleyn play', the yearly re-enactment of Mary Magdalene's discovery of the empty tomb.

63 View of Hestercombe in 1700. In the foreground is the private chapel established by Sir John de Meriet in 1316. It was demolished by Coplestone Warre Bampfylde in 1766.

Popular piety was expressed not only by church attendance. A few richer families went to the trouble of setting up their own private chapels, or oratories, notable examples being the chapels founded by the Meriets at Hestercombe in 1316 and by the Fraunceis family at Combe Florey in 1454. Less wealthy people could at least help to beautify their parish churches, and the worship conducted in them, by gifts in money and in kind. Amongst scores of examples, John Caldbeck, the vicar of Wellington, left his church a service book in 1498; money to buy a cope for Wilton church was given in 1511 by the will of Harry Lawrens; and in 1533 Roger Maynerd left money for gilding the high cross in the church at Creech St Michael. There were frequent bequests to building funds, and a great many for the maintenance of lights, such as that which in the 1530s burned before the image of the Virgin Mary in the north aisle at Pitminster.

Religious faith found expression also in the rituals of death. When Walter Dolyng, a Taunton merchant, made his will in 1492, he provided for mass to be said forever in Taunton Priory 'for me, my wif, our fadres and modres and all our children and all our good dears'. Six poor people clothed in black, each holding a candle, were to be present at his funeral, as were the prior and sub-prior, the canons and the novices. He gave 40s. for mending the road from Taunton to Blackbrook, and to his sister Margaret he left a rosary.

THE POWER of the church was already under threat long before Henry VIII's break with Rome in the 1530s. By the end of the 14th century, heretical preachers were active in the area of Bristol, and in the years that followed growing numbers of people, known as Lollards, gathered secretly to hear the scriptures read in English. In 1441, Thomas Oke, a Taunton brewer, was accused of possessing heretical books, and there is little doubt that at least some others in the town were also inclined to heresy.

The most striking fact, however, is that so many stayed faithful, and continued until the very eve of the Dissolution to lavish money on their parish churches. Between about 1522 and 1540 a new chancel was built for Bishops Hull church, and in the 1530s money was being given for Hillfarrance's splendidly sturdy west tower, as well as for the tower at Ruishton. When the lesser monasteries, including the priories of Barlynch and Cannington, were dissolved in 1536, riots in Taunton and Bridgwater evidently reflected outraged local feeling. Three years later, however, the visitation of Taunton Priory left no record of resistance. On Wednesday 12 February 1539, the last prior of Taunton, William Wyllyams, and the remaining priory canons gathered in the chapter house for perhaps the final time. There they signed the document by which the 'monastery or priory of Taunton' was surrendered to the king, and with it all the lands and rights the priory then possessed. By that simple means, a religious community which had survived in various forms for more than 700 years came quietly to an end. At the same time the people of Taunton Deane entered a period of change as decisive and transforming as any they had ever known.

64 The tower of St George's Church, Ruishton. Money was left for the building of the tower in 1530 and 1533. At the Dissolution of Taunton Priory in 1539, however, work was evidently given up and the tower stands today without its crown.

4

Tudors and Stuarts

65 Alabaster fragment of a crucifixion scene, *c.*1500, believed to have come from the church of SS Peter and Paul, Bishops Hull.

FOR AS LONG as Henry VIII survived, the progress of the English Reformation was slow. In 1536, the king ordered that the observance of many minor holy days should be abolished, and in 1538 the burning of lights before the images of saints was forbidden. But in most respects, English parish churches remained undisturbed. At Trull, in 1536 and 1540, the churchwardens bought frankincense for use at the continuing celebrations of the mass, and in 1542 money was spent for 'the dressynge of the ymagis' which the church then still contained. Trull's parish guild or brotherhood also flourished, raising money for the church by way of the merry-makings known as church ales, and a chantry priest at Trull was praying for the souls of the departed as late as 1547.

That was the year in which Edward VI succeeded his father, and in which the full force of the Protestant Reformation at last became apparent. At Trull, as in other churches, the great carved crucifix, or rood, and its flanking figures of St Mary and St John, were taken down from their place of honour above the chancel screen. Images were destroyed, stone altars were replaced by wooden tables, and ceremonies such as the Palm Sunday processions were abolished. Even the guilds and chantries quickly succumbed. The chantry chapel at Wiveliscombe had in any case been in use for some time as a store room, and the people of Milverton saw the abolition of their own chantry chapel as a welcome opportunity to buy lead from the roof for making water pipes.

When, during the brief reign of the Catholic Queen Mary, the Reformation changes were reversed, there is at least some local evidence that Protestantism was already taking root. In 1554, John Laverence of Trull mockingly offered to provide timber so the parish could set up the image of a 'great knave' in place of their former rood; John Penye of Wellington showed his contempt for the Catholic mass by holding a dog above his head at the high altar, in imitation of the elevation of the host, and proclaiming 'Lowe, here ys your god'; and John More, the rector of West Monkton, utterly refused to abandon his new wife, as Catholic doctrine now demanded. He bravely insisted that they would 'never depart before their death'. Many parishes were slow to replace the Latin mass books, vestments and furnishings they had disposed of such a short time before, though at Combe Florey they at least offered an excuse: their chalice, cope, service books and holy water bucket, they explained, had all been 'stolyne by robberye'.

The return to Catholicism did not survive the accession of Elizabeth I in 1558. For a second and final time the outward signs of Roman Catholicism were removed from parish churches, and a revised prayer book was issued setting forth the moderate Anglicanism to which most people quickly became loyal. Some refused to give up old allegiances. In 1591, the Muttleburys, a Catholic family from Ashill, paid a monthly fine of £20 rather than attend their parish church. Over much of the area around Taunton, however, it was not a lack of Protestant zeal, but an excess of it, which increasingly concerned Somerset's religious and civil authorities.

By the beginning of the 17th century, Puritan views, based especially on the teaching of Calvin, were already widespread, emphasising the authority of scripture, a dislike of ceremonial, and the importance of a godly life. In 1613, villagers from Stoke St Mary were among a growing number who abandoned their

parish churches to hear sermons and lectures delivered in Taunton by Puritan clergymen; the parish priest of Stoke St Gregory expressed alarm four years later because villagers were meeting to discuss complex questions of Calvinist theology, which, in his view, were only fit to be considered by 'judicious divines'; and in the 1630s, a Baptist congregation was said to be gathering secretly in woods near Taunton, possibly at Bickenhall.

66 The Rev. George Newton (1602–81). He was appointed vicar of St Mary's, Taunton, in 1631, and was the most influential Puritan clergymen in Taunton Deane before the Civil War. After the Restoration he became nonconformist minister of Paul's Meeting, Taunton, but at his death was brought back to St Mary's for burial.

Few issues divided Puritans more clearly from moderate Anglicans than the bitter disputes concerning parish revels and church ales. Since the late Middle Ages, such events had provided a popular means of raising money for the church. But they were increasingly condemned, not only because they frequently

67 Bench end in St Michael's Church, Milverton, *c.*1540, evidently depicting a man drinking ale.

resulted in violence and immorality, but because they took place on Sundays. A revel held at Bradford on Tone in 1610 was attended by 150 people from at least six parishes and was enlivened by a tennis match played in the churchyard. As was too often the case, however, good humour was short-lived, and a riot had broken out before the event came to an end. At West Hatch 11 years later, the church ale was disrupted by a violent quarrel between two villagers and was concluded by Michael Dyer being confined in the stocks.

Official attempts to control such occasions were frequently made but only partly successful. In 1594 and 1596 the Somerset justices prohibited the holding of all church ales and, in 1608, a similar prohibition was extended to include 'bulbaytings' and 'bearebaytings' such as those which took place

at the baiting site in the centre of Taunton. In 1633, Charles I inflamed Puritan opinion by confirming the right of his subjects to enjoy 'decent and sober recreations' on Sundays, and only with the Puritan triumph in the Civil War was there a decisive end to the controversy. Thereafter, ales and revels largely vanished from Somerset, though a few, at least, were defiantly continued. At Langford Budville in 1650 'a great rout of people', including visitors from Wellington, attended a parish revel complete with 'fiddling and dancing'; and on a Sunday at Staple Fitzpaine in 1655 the parishioners still managed to hold their 'play day' or revel. The event is recorded because Elizabeth Salter, like many before her, soon discovered that the pleasures of revel day had left her pregnant.

A PERIOD both more secular and more individualistic began with the Reformation, and the chief monuments of the years that followed were not the lavishly rebuilt churches of the late Middle Ages, but the new mansions of local gentry. At least a few of the Vale's gentry families, such as the Warres and the Stawells, had long enjoyed high status, as splendid medieval tombs at Kingston and Cothelstone have survived to prove. But the majority of such families in the Tudor and Stuart periods were recent recruits to gentry rank. They were largely descended from successful merchants and lawyers who had profited not only from the rapid inflation of prices after 1540 but from the lively market in land created by the break-up of monastic estates.

The houses built by these families were conspicuous expressions of social and economic advancement, and sometimes rose amidst the very ruins of the old order. Thomas More, a Taunton merchant and minor gentleman, built his mansion soon after 1552 on the site of Taunton Priory, evidently following the destruction of the priory complex shortly before. In the same way, the priory's grange farm at Pitminster and Corfe provided the

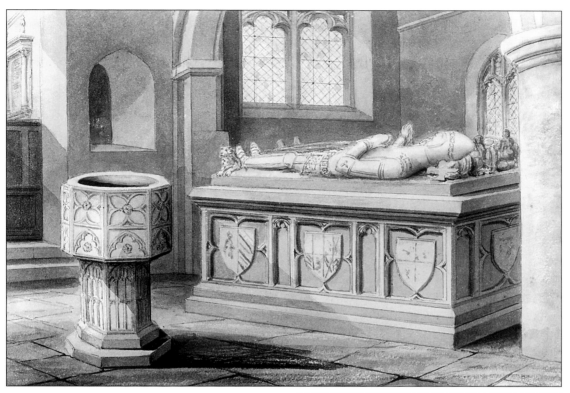

68 Interior of the Church of St Thomas of Canterbury, Cothelstone, by J. Buckler, 1843. The tomb is that of Sir Matthew de Stawell (d.1379) and his wife Eleanor.

69 Poundisford Park, Pitminster, c.1916. The house was begun by William Hill in about 1546 within the southern half of the bishop of Winchester's former deer park. The south front of the house is shown shortly before the removal of the courtyard wall and gateway.

70 Mansion of the Farewell family at Bishops Hull, by J. Buckler, 1837. The house was built in 1586 by George Farewell, whose ambitious alabaster monument is in the parish church.

71 Children of George Farewell (d.1609) depicted on his monument in the church of SS Peter and Paul, Bishops Hull. Nikolaus Pevsner praised the group as having been carved 'quite exceptionally beautifully'.

site for the new home of Humphrey Colles, a lawyer of Gray's Inn. He acquired the farm in 1543, and soon after, in the setting of monastic barns and fishponds, created the great house later known as Barton Grange.

Across the fields at Poundisford, two other major houses also rose in that period, both built on land leased from the bishop of Winchester. Poundisford Lodge and the more ambitious Poundisford Park were respectively the work of the Taunton merchant Roger Hill and his son William, and unlike Barton Grange have survived in fine completeness to the present day. So too has the slightly later mansion at Bishops Hull built in 1586 by George Farewell, and the partially rebuilt Cothelstone Manor, home of the Stawells. But perhaps the grandest of all the houses in the Vale of Taunton, the Popham mansion at Wellington, is among those of which no visible trace remains. The house was built by Sir John Popham (1533-1607), a judge noted for his brilliance and severity. He served successively as Speaker of the Commons, Attorney General and Lord Chief Justice, and in 1588 sent the first news to London that the Spanish Armada had been sighted. His mansion did not long survive a Royalist siege in the Civil War, but excavation has revealed a building 142 feet long (only 24 feet shorter than Montacute).

In no local family were the social, economic and religious changes of the 16th century more fully reflected than in the Portmans. They had been among Taunton's leading merchants at least since the early 14th century, and had frequently represented the borough in Parliament. A fortunate marriage in the mid-15th century brought them the estate at Orchard which became their chief Somerset home, and the legal profession, as so often, provided the means by which they rose to more than local prominence. John Portman flourished as a London lawyer in the early 16th century and was buried in the Temple Church when he died in 1521. But it was his son William (c.1498-1557) who was able to seize the far greater opportunities for advancement which arose in the 30 years following his father's death. In 1535 he was one of the commissioners appointed to value the possessions of Taunton Priory, and after the Dissolution was quick to acquire a substantial Somerset estate, largely created from former monastic land. He was responsible as well for purchasing the fields at Marylebone, near London, from which the immense wealth of his Victorian descendants was destined to flow. He was knighted in 1547, reached the very top of his profession in 1555 as Lord Chief Justice, and two years later was attended to his grave in London by all the Inns of Court. The 'large faire house' he built at Orchard Portman—finally demolished in about 1843—was at first no grander than its near neighbour Poundisford Park. But Sir William's prudent land investments, and the accidents of political history, ensured that for more than a century after his death neither the house nor its owners were ever far from the centre of West Country events.

72 Sir William Portman (c.1498-1557). He rebuilt Orchard House at Orchard Portman and was appointed Lord Chief Justice in 1555.

In the 17th century especially, numerous lesser gentlemen also achieved influence and prosperity, many of them marking their upward rise by attendance at Oxford University and the acquisition of a much-coveted coat of arms. A few even aspired to service as JPs on the county bench. Such men included members of the Beresford and Browne families of Taunton, the Mallacks and Powells of Wilton, the Lancasters of Milverton, the Dobles of Stoke St Mary, the Celys of Creech St Michael, and their longer-established neighbours, the Cuffes of Charlton Manor. Like the greater gentry, these families had found the means of thriving as landlords, merchants and commercial farmers in volatile economic and political conditions. But those same conditions ensured that, by the end of the 17th century, the Vale was far more socially stratified than 150 years earlier, and that the gulf which had opened between the prosperous and the poor was wider than it had ever been.

WHEN THOMAS GERARD visited Taunton Deane in 1633, he found a landscape memorable both for its beauty and its agriculture, and a town as 'faire and pleasant' as any he had seen. He followed a path which bordered the River Tone, remarking with approval on the 'many faire orchards', the flourishing cherry gardens, and the fertile soil which produced an abundance of fruit and other crops. He noted with admiration the thriving condition of Taunton's Saturday market, which was now so dominant in West Somerset that it was 'constantly served by 140 butchers'; and he commended the beauty of the Taunton streets, where 'springs of most sweet water' continually ran. It was evident to Gerard, as to most other visitors, that the chief engine of the local economy was the manufacture and sale of woollen cloth. But in the midst of the prosperous market town, and surrounded by a landscape whose farming reputation was already proverbial, it was agriculture which chiefly inspired his praise.

The effects of the Black Death in the 14th century, and the abandonment of demesne farming by the bishops of Winchester after 1418, had been decisive for the development of local agriculture. Land became relatively abundant, feudalism decayed, and communal patterns of farming were quickly given up. By the time John Leland visited the area in 1537 or 1538, he found a landscape 'al in Hegge rowes of Enclosures' with no remaining sign of the open fields, communally farmed, which had existed during the 14th century. Farms nevertheless remained small in size. In 1543-4, over half the farms in the Hundred of Holway were between ten and twenty acres in extent, and only a handful were more than fifty acres. Given the natural fertility of the best land in the Vale, these modest holdings were sufficient to supply local needs when harvests were good. Farming methods which, by the standards of the day, were relatively advanced, also helped. In 1609, John Norden expressed great admiration for the agricultural practices he observed in 'Tandeane', commending the 'extraordinary pains' taken by local farmers to prepare their land for sowing, and their equally determined efforts to ensure proper drainage.

As in the Middle Ages, mixed farming prevailed in the neighbourhood of Taunton. By the late 17th century, probate inventories show that the typical small farmer held about twenty acres, and, in addition to one or two horses, would often own a small herd of cattle, amounting to five or six animals, as well as a few pigs and sheep. Poultry was also frequently kept. Only on rough grazing land, such as that provided by the Quantock foothills at Kingston or the Blackdowns at Otterford, were larger sheep flocks usually to be found, though Edward Cely the younger proved the exception by keeping 90 sheep at Charlton in 1677.

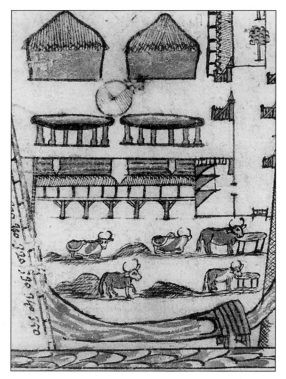

73   Detail from a map of Roughmoor Farm, Bishops Hull, 1718, showing cattle feeding, staddles and thatched ricks. The farm was held at that date by Edward Jarman, a tenant of the bishop of Winchester.

74 The Market Cross, Milverton, by W.W. Wheatley, 1849. The cross and its surrounding structure stood at the junction of Fore Street, Sand Street and St Michael's Hill. It was demolished in 1851.

Wheat was preferred above barley as the major grain crop, and peas and beans were extensively grown. The cider presses and vats for brewing beer, recorded in so many 17th-century inventories, point to an enduring feature of the local diet, and cheese-making was also important as a by-product of dairying. In 1679, John Crosse of Langaller died the owner of no fewer than 72 cheeses. In the area of West Hatch and Staple Fitzpaine, as well as at Milverton, limeburning was another important adjunct of farming activity, the burnt lime being used chiefly as a dressing to fertilise the fields and keep them clean, as well as for making limewash and mortar.

Trade in agricultural produce was conducted through the fairs and markets of the district. Many fairs, created by royal charter, originated in the 13th and 14th centuries, though not all of them survived the Middle

Ages. Fairs granted at Thurlbear, Staple Fitzpaine, Creech St Michael and Hatch Beauchamp, for example, vanished quickly—if they were ever held at all—and only those at Taunton, Otterford, Bishops Lydeard, Lydeard St Lawrence, Broomfield, Milverton, Wiveliscombe and Wellington achieved much lasting significance. Taunton, as usual, was pre-eminent. The bishop's records for the borough fair of St Botolph show that most of its trade during the 17th century was in horses and cattle, and that some traders came from considerable distances to attend. In 1625, Miles Nickoll and Richard Lezant travelled from Glamorganshire to sell their cattle, and several others came from parishes in Devon, Dorset and Wiltshire.

Annual fairs, however popular, never competed in economic significance with the Vale's weekly markets. By 1609, Wellington's

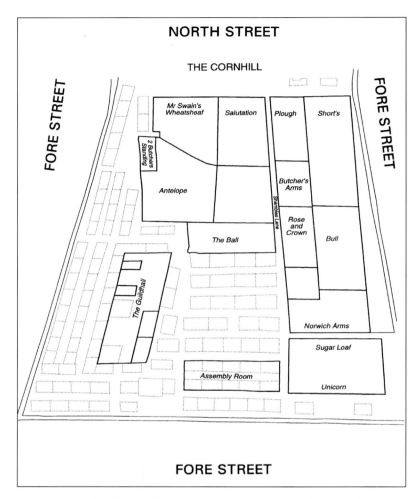

75 Plan showing the island site at the centre of Taunton before it was cleared in 1769 to make room for the Market House and the Parade. Half the site was occupied by 12 public houses which were divided by Shambles Lane. The Guildhall of 1467 was in the south-western area of the site; near the southern edge was the pillared market house, with assembly room above, built in the 1680s. Dotted lines indicate the locations of market standings.

market was held in the High Street each Thursday, a day when thirsty market-goers had 'great resort' to the Wellington alehouse of John Weaver. Taunton's market was held on Saturday, and throughout the Tudor and Stuart periods maintained an easy dominance in West Somerset. So great was its trade in 1673 that business was sometimes carried on till almost one in the morning, encouraging rowdy 'drinking and tippling' in nearby inns and ale-houses. The justices responded by ordering that the market should in future be closed no later than 10 o'clock at night.

As in the Middle Ages, the two borough portreeves were the officers chiefly responsible for supervising the markets and in particular

for granting leases of market standings. Other officers of the borough court leet recorded by the 16th century included the searchers and sealers of leather, who inspected all leather that was sold; two keepers of the greenskins, who inspected animal hides before they were tanned; two Cornhill keepers, who regulated the corn market; and two shambles keepers, who super-vised the sale of meat and later served also as ale tasters. In addition, rhine ridders ensured that the borough's water supply was not fouled or obstructed; aldermen were appointed to have oversight for the court leet within each of the borough's six tithings; and the borough constables and watchmen endeavoured to keep the peace.

T HE ECONOMIC SIGNIFICANCE of the woollen cloth industry in Taunton Deane reached its height in the 16th and 17th centuries. Throughout that period some clothmaking was still carried on by small-scale independent manufacturers, who owned the wool and yarn they worked with. But increasingly an elite group of local clothiers and merchants contracted with a multitude of much poorer spinners and weavers to supply the labour the industry required. Glimpses of such arrangements are sometimes preserved. In the 1660s Elias Martin of Ruishton rented a room in High Ham so he could 'put forth wool to spinning' within the parish. John Somers, a clothier from Clayhidon in the Devon Blackdowns, had a 'spininge howse' near Bradford on Tone in 1683. And Susanna Light of Hatch Beauchamp was struggling in 1676 to obtain from Andrew Groves, a Taunton sergemaker, the 17s. he owed her for spinning worsted wool.

Weaving was contracted out in a similar way. John Smith, a clothier from Haydon near Taunton, employed George and Edward Foweracres to weave broadcloth for him in 1650, but began to suspect they were stealing his yarn when the cloth 'came not home full weight, length, and breadth'. By 1704 an observer reported that 8,500 people were employed weekly in the Taunton cloth industry; and even if that figure is exaggerated, it suggests how pervasive and important cloth manufacture had become. In villages

76-9 Drawings by William Bidgood, 1879, showing the processes of carding, combing, spinning and weaving as traditionally carried out in Taunton Deane. Shorter wool sorted from fleeces was carded to make woollen cloth; longer wool was combed to make worsted cloth.

throughout Taunton Deane the racks where cloth was dried and stretched were a familiar sight (as is apparent from common field names such as 'Rack Orchard'), and in Taunton itself land beside the River Tone was given over to the drying racks of local manufacturers. The urban workers in the cloth trade mostly occupied poor housing in the East Reach area of the town, and over Taunton as a whole, an 18th-century writer noted, hung the 'very disagreeable' smell of the oil used to prepare the wool for spinning.

During the Tudor period, the local textile industry was dominated by white broadcloth, a very thick cloth which was heavily felted through the fulling process. In the 1580s, however, Benedict Webb began to manufacture a lighter, higher quality material in Taunton called 'Spanish' cloth or 'medley'. It made use of fine, dyed wool (often Spanish), and immediately found buyers in London. By the early years of the 17th century Spanish cloth had evidently become the chief textile product of Taunton Deane, and throughout the region helped to revive an industry always vulnerable to changes of fashion and to unpredictable stoppages in trade.

Taunton's importance as a textile centre was acknowledged in 1617 when it became the staple town for the wool trade in Somerset, and by 1629 a yarn market had been established which opened at 8 o'clock in the morning during the spring and summer, and at 9 o'clock in autumn and winter. This same period was also marked, however, by intense hardship for the industry. In 1622, the borough constables reported that the decay of the cloth trade had greatly impoverished the town, and in the same year the Sheriff of Somerset warned that large numbers of unemployed clothworkers in the county as a whole were a threat to good order. The outbreak of war with Spain in 1655 severely affected the Taunton trade—now dominated by light but hard-wearing serges— and during the next 20 years a rival Irish cloth industry, partly dependent on West Country

emigrants, was a further challenge to Taunton's prosperity. By 1681, 500 unemployed sergemakers at Taunton were reported to be 'mutinous' and faced the immediate prospect of starvation by 'flocking up and down the adjacent parts with insolent and peremptory resolves'. When the market for serge entered serious decline in the 1690s, James Fontaine, a Huguenot refugee to Taunton, responded by making a glossy worsted cloth called calamanco, and was soon imitated by envious rivals. Those who continued to trade in serge, such as the Taunton merchant William Harvey, were soon left in no doubt that the market in cloth was changing rapidly. 'I would readily buy some serges of you', a Lyme Regis merchant wrote to Harvey in 1699, 'did I know where to sell them again to any advantage.'

Much of the cloth made by the Taunton industry was traded through Blackwell Hall, the chief London cloth market. But overseas commercial links were also very strong. As early as 1434, five Taunton merchants, probably connected with the cloth trade, were accused of taking a Genoese ship by force off Cape St Vincent, and in 1467 Alexander Tous and Richard Bevyn, both Taunton merchants, shipped 5,000 pieces of tin and 300 woollen cloths from Topsham in Devon. Brittany, Holland, Austria and Spain were all important destinations for Taunton cloth in the Tudor and Stuart periods, most of it being exported through Topsham or Lyme Regis. By the 1580s Taunton merchants were even trading on the west coast of Africa. In 1588 they dispatched a ship 'fraughte with merchandise' to the Guinea coast, where both crew and cargo were promptly seized. In 1592 a more certain African trade was briefly established by Letters Patent of Queen Elizabeth. She granted to Thomas Pope the elder, Thomas Pope the younger, William Dare, Thomas Dare and John Coggan sole rights for 10 years to exploit the Guinea trade 'from the northemost parte of the ryver of Nunoe to the southemoste parte of the Ryver called Magrabumbo'. The profits of the enterprise were to be divided equally among the queen, the king of Portugal, and the merchants themselves.

The generations of local merchants who profited so handsomely from the cloth trade sometimes remembered their indebtedness to the people of Taunton Deane. Thomas Pope built almhouses near Taunton's East Gate in 1590; Simon Saunders, who died in 1591, left money to supply the poor with woollen cloth; and in the early 17th century other almshouses were established in the town by the merchants Robert Henley and Richard Huish. As munificent as anyone was Robert Gray. Though he was born in Taunton, Gray, like Richard Huish, made his fortune in London. His brick almshouses in East Street, built next to the house where he was born, had just been completed when he died in 1635. Together with Gray's fine effigy in St Mary's Church, they survive today to remind us of the riches generated by woollen cloth and the central place of the cloth trade in the history of Taunton Deane.

80 Bench end at St Mary's Church, Bishops Lydeard, depicting a three-masted ship typical of the late 15th century. A vessel of this kind was capable of being used either as a fighting ship or for trade.

81 Gray's Almshouses, East Street, Taunton, by H. Sheppard Dale, 1894.

THE LOCAL INFLUENCE of the bishops of Winchester declined yet further during the 16th and 17th centuries, but the ancient system of administration which operated in their name had not yet been superseded. The bishops' infaring tenants still attended at the Exchequer Chamber, above the gateway to Taunton Castle, to register property transfers or raise mortgages on land, and the manorial courts still dealt with minor breaches of the law and manorial custom, as well as with cases of debt. The courts for the infaring and outfaring hundreds generally met in the Great Hall of Taunton Castle, those for the borough in the 15th-century Guildhall. Documents created by these courts survive voluminously from 1507 onwards, and provide for the first time a detailed picture of communities contending with founderous roads, noisome dungheaps, dishonest tradesmen, and houses sometimes so dilapidated that they threatened to fall down. In 1508, the millers of Kingston, Corfe and South Trendle were all taking excessive tolls from their customers, as were many of their fellow millers throughout the period. Alehouse keepers, such as Ralph Sampson of East Reach in 1517, habitually sold ale from illegal measures, and bakers were often no less deceitful. Rotting entrails and animal dung fouled the river at Tone Bridge in 1540, and in the same year the poor and crowded housing outside the East Gate counted 'vagabonds and harlots' among its many inhabitants.

The government of the town was reformed in 1627 when a royal charter granted Taunton its first mayor and corporation, and so for the first time gave the borough an administrative body clearly independent of the bishop. The charter was declared void in 1661, soon after the Restoration of Charles II. But in 1677 the king was persuaded to grant a new charter despite the notorious reputation for disloyalty the town acquired during the Civil War. The rival administration set up by the charters further eroded the authority of the borough courts as the 17th century progressed, and the power of

82   Officers of the borough court leet with John White, Lord of the Manor of Taunton Deane, 1996. The bishops of Winchester, whose lordship suffered its only serious interruption between 1647 and 1662, finally sold the manor in 1822. The lordship was later acquired by H. Byard Sheppard (d.1928), grandfather of Mr. White.

83   Houses at Staplegrove, by Harry Frier, 1892.

the bishops' courts in general was being challenged by the rise of the justices of the peace.

The justices, presiding in Quarter Sessions, were Somerset's chief administrators and law enforcers by the time the 17th century began, and their records are a further source of vivid detail concerning the life of Taunton Deane. Problems associated with a tide of poverty were among those which most preoccupied the justices. Parish overseers, first appointed by the justices in 1572, bore the daily burden of relieving the poor, and at Staplegrove in 1599 rated the parish in order to pay small weekly pensions to 10 deserving paupers. But periodic crises of poverty, resulting from overpopulation, economic recession, harvest failures or the plague, demanded intervention from the justices themselves. When, in 1653, a rapid increase in population left the poor of St James's parish 'ready to perishe for want', the justices were petitioned to provide urgent help. The following year a similar plea came from Milverton where the poor were becoming a 'great and almost insupportable burthen' to the rest of the town's inhabitants. Outbreaks of

plague tested the justices even more severely. After plague reached Taunton in 1625, they ordered 'boothes or tents' to be set up at Bathpool 'for sequestringe and keepinge in of persons either infected or suspected to come from London'. Watchmen ensured that the order was obeyed and all trade with the capital was forbidden. A renewed outbreak in 1646-7 reached Taunton, Hillfarrance, North Petherton and Wiveliscombe, and forced the justices to levy emergency rates on unaffected parishes as well as to use the mansions at Orchard Portman and Hestercombe as pest houses.

84   Poor box of 1634 in the church of SS Peter and Paul, Combe Florey.

85   Houses at Norton Fitzwarren, by Harry Frier, 1892.

The justices had many less exceptional though often very onerous responsibilities. They licensed alehouses, saw to the maintenance of major bridges, and approved the binding-out of poor apprentices, rescuing many from subsequent ill-treatment by their masters: in 1631 John Nashion was discharged from his apprenticeship in Bishops Lydeard when the 'ill usage and merciless dealinge' he had suffered became known; and in 1653 the justices also discharged John Oland, apprentice to a Taunton weaver, after he was left 'almost starued to death and eaten out with lice'. The financial consequences of bastardy were also a perennial concern. In 1608, the reputed father of an illegitimate child at West Buckland was ordered to contribute to its maintenance by paying the churchwardens nine pence every Sunday 'at or upon the communion table of the church',

while the mother was to contribute a further seven pence. In addition, both were to confess their misdeeds in West Buckland church or, if they refused, to suffer a public whipping. No such choice was available to Agnes Bristell of Norton Fitzwarren in 1621. Having borne an illegitimate child, she was ordered to be whipped through the village street by the tithingman or his deputy.

The records of the justices are dominated above all by reports of assault, sexual misconduct, and theft. Cases can be found for almost every parish in the Vale during the 17th century, and include accounts of attempted murder, poaching expeditions in Neroche Forest, the activity of pickpockets on the streets of Taunton, and many illicit sexual adventures in taverns, outhouses and the open fields. The outcome of such cases is usually unrecorded. At least some offenders endured the public humiliation of the stocks, such as the five men at Taunton observed in the stocks one Sunday in the summer of 1653.

Others were sent to the house of correction which stood close to Taunton's medieval town bridge. The building was 'much ruinated' in 1608 and its roof 'altogether decayed' in 1632, but it was nevertheless a place of confinement far preferable to the two borough lock-ups on the ground floor of the Guildhall. They were known respectively as 'the Cow House' and 'the Little Ease' and were so 'horrid and shocking' that in the 18th

century the vagrants and deserters who were chiefly imprisoned there were known to take their own lives in despair. For a few, the end of the judicial process was death by hanging, usually at the long-established execution site at Stone Gallows, south-west of Bishops Hull. When Thomas Gerard passed close by in 1633 he did not think the gruesome place worthy of remark. Instead, in the midst of a century which would supply too many examples of violent death, he fixed his eyes on the natural beauties that surrounded him and the 'most pleasant and delectable walke' by which he made his way to Taunton.

86 Huntsman depicted on a 16th-century bench end in St Laurence's Church, Lydeard St Lawrence, by W.W. Wheatley, 1845. Hunting expeditions, chiefly illicit, are copiously recorded in 17th-century Quarter Sessions records. Staple Park in Staple Fitzpaine and Neroche Forest were frequent destinations.

5

Rebellion

STEPHEN TIMEWELL, the Royalist mayor of Taunton, woke early on 11 May 1683. By 3 o'clock in the morning, he had risen from his bed and was walking through the town in expectation of trouble. Rather to his surprise, he found Taunton 'indifferent peaceable' for most of the long day, with 'only several persons unknown to me with their hats cocked up and orange ribbons therein'. At about 5 o'clock in the afternoon, however,

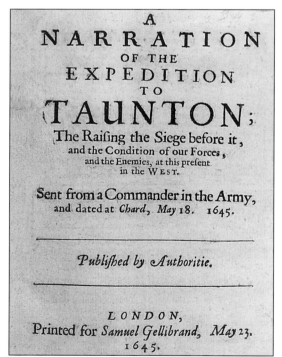

A
NARRATION
OF THE
EXPEDITION
TO
TAUNTON;
The Raiſing the Siege before it,
and the Condition of our Forces,
and the Enemies, at this preſent
in the WEST.

Sent from a Commander in the Army,
and dated at *Chard, May* 18. 1645.

Publiſhed by Authoritie.

LONDON,
Printed for *Samuel Gellibrand, May* 23.
1645.

87 Civil War tract describing the raising of the second siege of Taunton, May 1645.

crowds began to gather in the High Street, and by the time the mayor reached the scene more than 1,000 people were there, shouting, clapping their hands, and throwing their hats into the air. A riot broke out, and Timewell only saved himself by a hasty retreat. He could do nothing to quell the wild behaviour of the crowd that night; nor could anything prevent the building of a bonfire which, early the following morning, became a focus for defiant celebrations.

The cause of those celebrations, by then long-established as an annual event, was well known to every inhabitant of Taunton Deane. For it had been on 11 May 1645, near the brutal climax of the First Civil War, that the Royalist siege of Taunton had been raised, and that the town, against every reasonable expectation, had regained its freedom. Thirty-eight years later, as Timewell surveyed the results of one night's rioting, neither he nor other Somerset loyalists could be in any doubt that Taunton remained 'the sink of all the rebellion in the West'.

TAUNTON'S WILLINGNESS to defy authority had found early expression in the support it gave to Perkin Warbeck at the close of the Middle Ages. Not until the early 17th century, however, did the town begin to acquire its wider reputation as a centre of opposition to the king and a stronghold in which Puritan beliefs were free to flourish. By the 1630s the Puritan zeal of local people had

88   View of Taunton from the north-east by C. Haseler, early 19th century.

brought them into serious conflict with the religious policies of Charles I and of his archbishop, William Laud; at the same time the king's attempts to extract arbitrary taxes in the form of Ship Money were quickly becoming another cause of deep antagonism. Taunton had a higher assessment for Ship Money than any other Somerset town in 1635, and three years later, when the hated tax was levied again, hundreds bluntly refused to pay. Local farmers disposed of their stock so that it could not be seized by the sheriff's officers, and Thomas Saunders, a constable of the hundred, was arrested for failing to hand over even the small sum he had managed to collect. When, in August 1642, the Civil War between the forces of the king and Parliament finally broke out, the allegiances of Taunton, and of many villages surrounding it, were already beyond doubt.

Together with Wellington and Dunster, the town was quick to declare itself for Parliament and at once became an island of resistance in a region generally loyal to the king. In September 1642, when a retreating Royalist force made quarters at Bradford on Tone, church bells were rung backwards and warning fires burned in the darkness to express the defiance and alarm of local people. A Parliamentary force briefly secured Taunton later that month and collected at least £10,000 for Parliament's cause; but the Royalist effort to capture the town was not long delayed. In June 1643 the Marquess of Hertford, together with Prince Maurice and Sir Ralph Hopton, arrived from Chard with a Royalist force, and having made headquarters at the Portman mansion in Orchard Portman he sent a summons into Taunton ordering surrender. Though the townsmen were defiant, the garrison fled, and on 5 June Taunton was bloodlessly captured together with 1,000 arms, 22 barrels of gunpowder, and seven or eight pieces of ordinance.

The king's supremacy in Somerset lasted more than a year, and might have continued indefinitely but for the actions of Laurence Chislett, a Taunton man from St James's parish. Chislett was held prisoner at Taunton for 20 weeks by its Royalist governor Sir John Stawell; but in the summer of 1644 he made his escape and brought news to Parliamentary generals then meeting in Lyme Regis that Taunton's garrison of 800 men had been reduced to no more than eighty. Using Chislett as their guide, a Parliamentary force entered the town secretly at the beginning of July, and within a few days the garrison had surrendered. Royalist carelessness in allowing Taunton's capture proved very costly, not least because the new governor of the town, chosen in Parliament's name, was Robert Blake, a man remarkable both for his courage and for his outstanding powers of leadership.

89 Robert Blake (1599-1657), the Parliamentary defender of Taunton during the Civil War sieges of 1644-5.

Blake realised at once that his hold on Taunton, a key to the West, would not go unchallenged, and in a flurry of preparation his forces and the people of the district made themselves ready for the coming storm. Coin hoards, such as those discovered at West Hatch, Stoke St Mary, and in East Reach, were hastily buried, and the long gallery of the Portman mansion became the hiding place for £200 in silver. Taunton was almost without physical defences except where the river bordered it to the north, and the castle, whose ancient keep tower was by now in decay, provided the only stronghold. Trenches and barricades were made at the East Gate, where the road from Bridgwater and Bristol entered the town, and other defences appeared near St Mary's Church and outside the castle east gate. But nothing, in the short time available, could greatly alter Taunton's extreme vulnerability.

The first of the Royalist sieges of Taunton began in October 1644 when Colonel Edmund Wyndham arrived before the town and made headquarters at Orchard House. He positioned cannon to command the East Gate and the castle, and his forces, over 3,000 strong, attacked repeatedly. But Blake was defiant in spite of the enemy's greatly superior numbers, refusing to submit even when the Royalists stormed the town and forced the defenders to retreat to the castle compound. 'We neither feare your menaces nor accept your proferrs', Blake wrote to Wyndham in reply to an offer of surrender terms. When, shortly afterwards, Wyndham learned that a Parliamentary relief force was approaching, he gave up the siege and conceded an improbable victory to Blake by withdrawing to Bridgwater. Taunton's rescuers finally arrived on 14 December and thought its survival almost miraculous, 'their works being for the most part but pales and hedges, and no line about the town'.

Once more, Blake knew that respite would be short-lived, and defensive preparations in the New Year of 1645 were correspondingly prodigious. It was evidently now that Blake's

90 St Mary's Vicarage, Taunton, a building whose earliest features appear to be of the 16th or early 17th century. 'The Vicar's House' was heavily fortified by Robert Blake during his defence of Taunton.

91 Orchard House, Orchard Portman, by J.C. Buckler, 1832. The Elizabethan mansion of the Portman family repeatedly served as head-quarters for the Royalist forces who laid siege to Taunton during the Civil War.

men may have completed a full circuit of defences by constructing more than 2,000 yards of earthen banks, the whole length being faced with earth-filled wicker cylinders and topped with brushwood. Years later, Richard Hillard of Taunton recalled how he was one of the many who lay on the defences 'day and night through wet and cold' waiting for the Royalists to attack. The renewed assault came early in 1645, when the king's forces returned to Taunton and again made their headquarters at Orchard Portman. The brutal indiscipline of the Royalist troops, chiefly commanded by Lord Goring and Sir Richard Grenville, gave warning of the horrors to come, not only for Taunton but for the Vale as a whole. Reports soon reached London of villages laid waste, of repeated plundering and horrific rapes, and of local men forced to hide themselves in 'woods and holes' to avoid

summary hanging. By 10 April a besieging army of 6,000 men had approached within musket shot of the town's defences, and so intense was the Royalist bombardment that Taunton appeared sometimes 'as if besieged by a wall of fire'. At Wellington that month a Parliamentary garrison occupying the old Popham mansion, Wellington House, was swiftly overcome and savagely dispatched. But the defenders of Taunton were both more numerous and more obstinate, only too aware that the fall of the town would mean 'certain butchery'.

The town's water supply was cut off, the mill stream diverted, and by the beginning of May Blake and his garrison confronted an army which, by the addition of many pressed men, had grown to eight thousand. To all but the defenders themselves defeat seemed inevitable when the last and most determined

92 *Above left.* George, Lord Goring (1608-57), one of the commanders of the Royalist assaults on Taunton. Goring was an able but impetuous soldier who suffered crushing defeat at the Battle of Langport in July 1645.

93 *Above right.* Sir Ralph Hopton (1598-1652), who led the final Royalist assault on Taunton in May 1645. No Royalist commander was more greatly respected by his opponents than Hopton.

Royalist onslaught began on 6 May. A defence work near St Mary's Church was quickly abandoned in the face of heavy bombardment, and in the course of the next two days the attackers captured the whole of East Reach and began to force a way beyond the East Gate into the heart of Taunton itself. Desperate fighting followed on 9 May, inspired on both sides by the knowledge that a Parliamentary relief force was already marching westward. 'You Roundhead rogues', the attackers called out, 'you look for relief, but we have relieved them ... We will not leave a house standing if you do not yield.'

East Street was taken in the face of fierce resistance, and as the flames of the burning town lit up the night sky, nothing remained to Blake but St Mary's Church, the castle compound, an entrenchment in the market place, and a defence work called the Maiden's

Fort. During the following two days Blake scornfully rejected terms of surrender, famously replying to one Royalist offer that he had four pairs of boots left and would eat three of them before he submitted. But the Royalists were almost successful in bribing disloyal townsmen to fire what little of Taunton remained in Blake's control. When the plot was discovered, three traitors, including one woman, were instantly killed by the garrison or the populace, and others were soon hanged.

After forced marches from Blandford, 7,000 Parliamentary troops commanded by Colonel Ralph Weldon at last descended from the Blackdown Hills above Pitminster on 10 May. As they neared the town a foot soldier called out to a cavalry officer, 'O brave horse, go on, show them no more mercy than to a louse', to which the officer replied, 'O fellow soldier, let us remember our God, and not

fight in malice, but do his work, and leave the success to him.' They quartered sleeplessly that night in the fields of Pitminster, Poundisford and Trull, and next morning, 11 May 1645, they prepared to fight.

The Royalists mistakenly believed that a force much larger than Weldon's had arrived, and were so thorough in blocking the roads with trees that it took 12 hours to march from Trull to Taunton. When at last Weldon's men entered the town, bringing 'unspeakable comfort to the distressed inhabitants', the Royalist army had already fled, leaving behind them awful scenes of suffering and devastation. Two-thirds of the town was in ruins, many hundreds were dead, and in the ravaged countryside surrounding Taunton the fields were as bare 'as if they had sowed salt'. Lord Goring returned to Taunton in June and made a final attempt to starve it into surrender. But on 3 July he marched away, destined a week later to suffer defeat at the Battle of Langport, the last major battle of the First Civil War. A year after taking possession of the town, Blake's courage and determination had triumphed: Taunton had survived.

94 View of Trull from King's Gatchell, by Miss Wigram, c.1910. Colonel Ralph Weldon's relieving force quartered near Trull on 10 May 1645.

95 The Bishop's Chamber, Taunton Castle, during re-roofing in 1884. The castle suffered severe bombardment from across the Mill Stream during the sieges of 1644-5.

THE TOWN'S DESPERATE STRUGGLE during the sieges of 1645 achieved national fame, and had major consequences for the outcome of the war. By keeping Lord Goring's forces engaged at Taunton, Blake and his garrison ensured that the king's army at the Battle of Naseby on 14 June was crucially depleted. But for the distraction provided by Taunton, the king might have won the battle and fought on. In the event, Naseby marked the final defeat of the Royalist cause.

The reckoning which now followed was heavy indeed for those who found themselves on the losing side. The Portman family were fined more than £6,000 for supporting the king, a sum which was 'bestowed upon the town of Taunton, towards recompence of their great losses and sufferings'. John Coventry of Barton Grange was also fined, and Sir John Stawell of Cothelstone, former Royalist governor of Taunton, endured a long imprisonment, first in

Newgate and then in the Tower of London. He estimated his losses at over £30,000, and learned helplessly from his steward how his estates at Cothelstone and Merridge were being despoiled, and how Cothelstone Manor House, robbed of its lead, had been reduced in part to a 'confused heape' of masonry.

Lesser men also suffered. Edward Clarke of Bradford on Tone, who commanded a company of Royalist infantry at the siege of Bridgwater, was imprisoned in Clerkenwell and fined £40; William Nosse of Lambrook Farm paid almost £500 for his part in the siege of Exeter; and Robert Ballifant of Bishops Lydeard, who only marched with the Royalist army to escape his debts, was made to pay £67.

Taunton and the Vale were never without Royalists, even when the sufferings inflicted in the king's name were still most bitterly remembered. 'Wandering loyalists' would gather at Nynehead during the Commonwealth

96   The Manor House, Cothelstone, by W.W. Wheatley, 1848. Its ruined wing was rebuilt in 1855.

for services taken by ejected Anglican clergy; men such as John Baylye of Shoreditch would publicly drink the king's health in local inns; and John Sawser of Bishops Lydeard was not alone in believing that the new governors of England 'were no other than dishmakers, tinkers, and cobblers'. But loyal voices were always few, and when, in May 1660, Charles II returned in triumph to London, the Vale's hostility to Royal government was almost as implacable as ever. The king felt no greater affection for Taunton people than they felt for him. He took away the borough charter, renewing it with important restrictions in 1677, removed the summer Quarter Sessions from the town, and ordered the destruction of Taunton Castle (though only the ancient keep tower seems in the end to have been dismantled).

Hundreds refused to accept the doctrines of the re-established Anglican church, and flocked instead to nonconformist conventicles. In 1669, when such meetings were briefly tolerated, 340 dissenters regularly worshiped in houses at North Curry, 60 at Lydeard St Lawrence, 400 at Wellington and West Buckland, and many more in such places as Stoke St Mary, Pitminster, Trull, West Monkton and Creech St Michael. But nowhere was the multitude greater than in Taunton itself. On Easter Day 1682 Mayor Timewell broke up a conventicle 2,000 strong, and the following year continued his government-approved persecution of dissenters by gutting the meeting-house used by the Baptists and the great Presbyterian meeting-house known as Poles (now Paul's Meeting). Galleries, pulpits, seats and doors were all torn out, and to the sound of church bells which rang through the night, they were burned in a great bonfire on the Cornhill. 'I have fought with thousands of the beasts of Ephesus,' Timewell wrote, 'and have overcome them.'

Such optimism was misplaced. In reality the disaffection of Taunton people was growing rapidly, especially as they contemplated the

likely succession to the throne of Charles II's Catholic brother, James, Duke of York. In July 1683 Sir Francis Warre and Lord Stawell arrived in Taunton to search for arms in the houses of suspected malcontents, and the same year William Burridge of St James's parish was heard to say that he would 'fight to his knees in blood' before he would accept a Catholic king. His own hopes for a Protestant succession, like the hopes of many others, now lay with the Duke of Monmouth, the King's favourite but illegitimate son.

Rumours of a planned rebellion began to fill the West Country almost as soon as James II succeeded to the throne in 1685. A letter to a Taunton man, intercepted in late May, explained that the arrival of a 'certain person' could be expected soon. Shortly afterwards a miller and his wife spoke of seeing 80 horsemen riding in the night past Obridge Mill, and by 3 June a member of Taunton corporation was in no doubt that 'the dissenting party had some wicked designe afoot'. The posts were searched in several West Country towns, and Exeter secured itself against strangers gathering for the fair. But there was as yet no real sign of trouble, and on 8 June a report from Taunton described the town as 'very peaceable and quiet'.

Vindication came swiftly for those loyalists who had feared the worst. Early on the morning of 12 June, news reached Sir Edward Phelips in Taunton that Monmouth had landed at Lyme Regis about sunset the day before. A servant of Sir William Portman's immediately rode south, returning from Lyme at 2 o'clock the following morning to report that Monmouth's army was some 1,500 strong. But already more recruits were marching through the lanes of Dorset and Somerset to swell the rebel numbers.

Monmouth led his forces into Chard on 16 June, reached Ilminster the following day, and on 18 June made for Taunton itself. The militia had abandoned the town early the previous morning, and the inhabitants, quickly

97 *Left*. James Scott, Duke of Monmouth and Buccleuch (1649–85), by Sir Peter Lely.

98 *Above*. Elizabeth Broadmead (1670–1785) at the age of 115, by Harry Frier after an earlier engraving. In 1685 she 'walked in procession before the Duke of Monmouth on his entering Taunton'.

seizing their opportunity, broke into St Mary's Church and carried away the militia arms that were stored there. When a clergyman protested at this action, a 'sour saucy fellow' responded with the words, 'The towne is ours now, and you shall know that we are uppermost.'

Monmouth was greeted with wild enthusiasm in the flower-strewn streets of Taunton, and the two full days he remained in the town marked the rebellion's highest point. He lodged at Captain John Hucker's house in East Street, and it was there on 19 June that the 27 'maids of Taunton' presented him with flags for his troops, and that Mary Blake, a schoolmistress, gave him a Bible and a naked sword. On 20 June a mob of 500 armed men forced members of the corporation to attend at the market cross to hear Monmouth proclaimed king. Then, on 21 June, his ill-trained army of yeomen and clothworkers, including at least 400 recruits from Taunton and many more

from the villages around, set out on their indecisive march into north Somerset. His forces held Norton St Philip against a royal army on 27 June. But defeat at Sedgemoor on 6 July was crushing.

James II began to exact his bloody revenge on West Country rebels almost at once, and by the time the Duke of Monmouth was executed in London on 15 July, Colonel Kirke, with his Tangier regiment, had already reached Taunton. Kirke had 19 of the rebels hanged, drawn and quartered outside the *White Hart Inn*, reputedly ordering 'the fifes to play, the trumpets to sound, and the drums to beat' to drown the cries of the dying men. Two months later, on 18 September, Judge Jeffreys opened the Bloody Assizes in the great hall of the castle and was faced with 514 prisoners for trial. Of these, 144 were condemned to hang (a sentence which for the most part was carried out) and 284 were sentenced to transportation.

99 *Above right.* The *White Hart Inn* at the junction of High Street and Fore Street, 1863. The building was demolished in 1968.

100 *Above right.* George Jeffreys (1648–89), architect of the Bloody Assizes, in a portrait of about 1680.

101 The great hall of Taunton Castle, *c.*1910.

102 Sir William Portman (1644-90), 6th baronet Portman. With his cousin, Sir Edward Seymour, he was one of the most powerful men in the West of England.

If, until that time, the sieges of the Civil War had formed Taunton's bitterest recollections of suffering, now the sight of trees 'loaden almost as thick with quarters as with leaves' provided a yet more enduring vision of horror. Even the Tory gentry, who had so notably failed to support Monmouth's cause, began to fear that the Catholic king was a threat both to their social position and their church; and when, in 1686, a group of Tory gentlemen, probably including Sir William Portman, gathered secretly in Dorset, their talk was no longer of loyalty to James but of a revolution which would give power to his Protestant son-in-law, William of Orange. Two years later, on 5 November 1688, a ship bearing the Prince arrived at Brixham, and the 'Glorious Revolution' had begun.

Any who feared that this enterprise would end as disastrously as Monmouth's were soon reassured. The Whig gentry of Devon overcame their initial caution, and by 15 November Somerset gentry, including Sir William Portman and Sir Francis Warre, had joined the Prince in Exeter. Taunton joyfully allowed 'three sorry-looking Dutchmen' to take possession of the town in the Prince's name, and by 11 December he was marching to London almost unopposed.

A period of unprecedented domestic peace and religious toleration now lay ahead, inaugurated in the New Year by the Convention Parliament which offered the throne to William and Mary as joint sovereigns. But even as the tragic conflicts of the 17th century receded into history, the people of Taunton could never forget the flames which had destroyed their town in 1645, or all those who, 40 years later, had been the pitiful victims of King James's judicial savagery.

6

The Age of Improvement

NEVER AGAIN did matters of belief and religious practice dominate the life of Taunton Deane as they had during the 17th century. In the century which followed, nonconformity, though still a powerful force, failed to inspire the destructive quarrels of earlier times, and the vigour of the Anglican church ebbed low. Secular concerns prevailed instead, encouraged particularly by peace at home and relative prosperity, as well as by a transport revolution which was opening Somerset to the influence of the greater world as never before. In the course of the 18th and early 19th centuries the face of Taunton Deane was transformed. Turnpike roads, canals and railways were successively added to the landscape; the urban scene was reshaped to reflect the tastes of increasingly numerous middle-class and professional families; and the gentry, grown wealthy from the profits of land ownership, commerce and the law, improved their estates and rebuilt their mansions.

Nothing in the 18th century affected the Vale more than the rapid transformation of its roads. Concern for the state of the roads was, of course, by no means new, and local justices in the 17th century had been zealous in requiring parishes to put their roads in order. At Milverton in 1630, for example, the justices took action after local people plundered the highway for soil and dung, leaving it full of 'divers pittes with risings and excesive fallings downe'; and in 1672, the roads through Thornfalcon—probably including the main route to Ilminster—were reportedly so ruinous that a rate was ordered to pay for repairs.

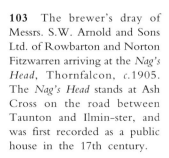

103 The brewer's dray of Messrs. S.W. Arnold and Sons Ltd. of Rowbarton and Norton Fitzwarren arriving at the *Nag's Head*, Thornfalcon, *c.*1905. The *Nag's Head* stands at Ash Cross on the road between Taunton and Ilmin-ster, and was first recorded as a public house in the 17th century.

But piecemeal action was never enough. Thomas Prowse, M.P. for Somerset from 1740 to 1767, announced to an amused House of Commons that the roads around Taunton could as easily be made navigable as fit for wheeled traffic. That opinion hardly exaggerated the conditions which faced local travellers, especially those who were forced to use the Vale's high-banked hollow ways during winter months or times of flood. As late as 1814, memories survived of two people who were swept to their deaths on the road from Staple Fitzpaine to Shoreditch because of the 'rapidity and depth of the water'.

The 18th century's response to the crisis of its roads was the creation of turnpike trusts, bodies authorised by Parliament to take control of major routes and to ensure their maintenance through the levying of tolls. The Taunton Turnpike Trust was established in 1752 and immediately began the process of remaking the roads which converged on the town. By October that year, James Upton was writing

104 Granite milestone with cast-iron plate outside Cothelstone Manor House. The road at this point formed part of the Bridgwater Turnpike Trust and was turnpiked from Enmore to Bishops Lydeard in 1759.

from Taunton to praise the achievements of the trustees and their engineer:

> They have now all round the town, for a full mile, the best roads I ever saw: and next year they go on as the Act of Parliament directs them viz to mend 7 miles in the great London road. There are some great strokes of art shewn, particularly in draining the water.

There were to be frequent future complaints about the administration of Somerset's turnpike trusts and the repair of roads in their care. But by 1800, the network of turnpikes created throughout the county provided a more efficient means of communication than had ever existed before. Writing in 1791, Joshua Toulmin, Taunton's first historian, remarked that since the building of the turnpikes the Taunton stage coach could make the journey to London in two days rather than four. And by 1822 the coach which ran from Whitmarsh's Coach Office next to the *Castle Inn* arrived from London in just 23 hours.

Traffic along the River Tone also developed rapidly during the 18th century—as it did on many English rivers—and was especially important in supplying Taunton and the Vale with coal for domestic hearths and for lime kilns. The Parrett and the Tone had been used for carrying goods between Bridgwater and Taunton at least since the 13th century. But the narrowness of the Tone at some points, and the frequent shallows which marked its course in dry weather, discouraged regular trade. Even more significant as obstacles were the medieval mills at Firepool, Obridge and Bathpool, together with the more distant mill at Ham in Creech St Michael. For much of the Middle Ages river traffic could reach no closer to the town than Ruishton or Bathpool Cross, though the construction of a primitive lock or 'cist' in about 1368 allowed Bathpool Mill to be negotiated when the river was high. The first serious attempts to keep the river navigable throughout the year were not made until the 17th century. In 1638, Charles I granted to John Malet of Enmore sole

105   Fore Street, Taunton, looking towards the Market House and the Parade, *c*.1850.

106   Bathpool Mill, West Monkton, *c*.1910.

navigation rights over the Parrett and Tone from Bridgwater to Bradford bridge. Malet improved the navigation at his own expense, levying tolls to pay for the work. But at his death much remained to be done, and by the end of the century sea coal destined for the town still had to be unloaded at Ham, the tidal limit of the River Tone, then carried expensively to Taunton on pack horses.

The rights to the Tone navigation were bought by a group of Taunton's leading inhabitants in 1698, and the following year an Act of Parliament created the body known as the Conservators of the River Tone. The Conservators were given powers to improve the course of the river, particularly from Ham Mills to Taunton, to build all necessary bridges, wharves, weirs and locks, and to levy tolls. As

107 Warehouses beside the River Tone below Coal Orchard, by Harry Frier, *c.*1890.

108 Firepool lock, Taunton, where the Bridgwater and Taunton Canal meets the River Tone, 1950. In the background is the pumping station built in 1889 to draw water from the canal for use by the Great Western Railway.

early as October 1699, a new lock was being installed at Obridge, and in June the following year the first boat was able to 'try all the locks' which had by then been constructed. A second Act in 1708 allowed further improvements to be made to the river channel, and by 1769 wharves near the town bridge were receiving coal from Swansea and Neath together with other goods such as iron, lead, oil and wine. In 1823, more than 28,000 tons of coal reached Taunton by river, while more than 800 tons, comprising mostly woollen cloth and agricultural produce, were exported in the opposite direction.

The heyday of the Tone navigation was short-lived. At the beginning of 1827 the first vessel was able to reach Taunton using a newly-completed canal between Huntworth and Taunton, and five years later the Conservators acknowledged commercial reality by selling their rights in the Tone to the Bridgwater and Taunton Canal Company. Thereafter, coal barges which unloaded at the Taunton wharves used the Tone only for the short journey from

Firepool, where the canal and the river met. The completion in 1838 of the Grand Western Canal between Firepool and the Devon border at Lowdwells allowed canal traffic to travel from Bridgwater as far west as Tiverton. In 1842 the building of the Chard Canal, which joined the Bridgwater and Taunton at Creech St Michael, also provided a route southward.

The canal age, in its turn, was already coming to an end by the time the Chard Canal was completed; for it was in July 1842 that Brunel's Bristol and Exeter Railway reached Taunton, the arrival of the first passenger train made memorable by the presence of the great engineer himself. The West Somerset Railway from Taunton was completed to Watchet in 1862 and to Minehead 12 years later; in 1866 a line was opened from Taunton to Chard; and in 1873 the Devon and Somerset Railway through Milverton and Wiveliscombe finally reached Barnstaple. Little more than a century had passed since the creation of the Taunton Turnpike Trust in 1752. During that time, however, the transport infrastructure of Taunton Deane, and of the county as a whole, had developed almost beyond recognition.

109 Aqueduct which carried the Grand Western Canal over the driveway to Nynehead Court. The aqueduct was built *c*.1838 by James Green and forms part of a fine group of canal structures at Nynehead, including the remains of a vertical canal lift.

110 Thorne Station, Thornfalcon, on the Chard branch of the Great Western (previously Bristol and Exeter) Railway, *c*.1910. The line was originally broad gauge but was converted to standard gauge during a single day in 1891.

THE HABITS of 'Improvement' which characterised so many aspects of the 18th and early 19th centuries were adopted with particular enthusiasm by gentry land-owners. Some introduced new agricultural methods on their home farms and encouraged tenant farmers to do the same. But local gentry devoted themselves most of all to the building or rebuilding of their own houses. A few existing houses had already been transformed shortly before the 18th century began. The Tudor mansion of the Portmans, two miles from Taunton, was greatly enlarged in classical style at some time before the death of Sir William Portman in 1690, and the Sanford mansion, Nynehead Court, underwent its own classical transformation in about 1675. It was in the 18th century, however, that the tide of architectural change rose particularly high.

After John Bampfylde acquired Hestercombe by marriage in 1718 he employed glaziers, stone cutters, carpenters and masons to build a Palladian front for his largely Tudor house; and at Bishops Lydeard the ambitious mansion first called Hill House and later Sandhill Park was being built for John Periam in 1728, when detailed accounts begin. From the 1730s onward new or rebuilt mansions began to rise throughout the Vale and included Combe Florey House (*c*.1730), Lydeard House (*c*.1740), Bagborough House (1745), Walford House (*c*.1745; rebuilt after a fire in 1780) and Hatch Court (*c*.1755).

The landscape settings of the Vale's 18th-century mansions were often designed with as much care as the houses themselves. That was particularly true once the craze for the 'picturesque' took hold after 1750. By the 1790s

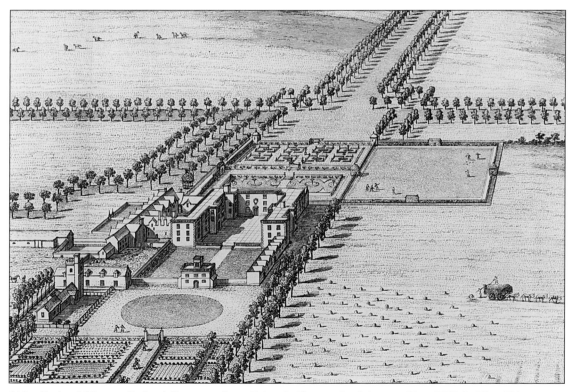

111 Orchard House, Orchard Portman, from *Britannia Illustrata* by Johannes Kip, 1707-8. The 17th-century additions to the house overshadow the original Tudor building. The mansion was finally demolished in about 1843, most of its site now being covered by Taunton racecourse.

112 Hatch Court, Hatch Beauchamp, by Thomas Bonnor, 1785. The mansion was at that date the home of the Collins family.

Hatch Court had been given a landscaped deer park complete with 'several temples and seats', while Sandhill possessed a deer park and a lake. The eccentric Thomas Slocombe of Tirhill near West Bagborough filled his extensive grounds with an array of classical statuary, and on the hill above the Manor House at Cothelstone Lady Hillsborough built a prospect tower commanding 'a view of almost unsurpassed grandeur over the Western shires'.

But nowhere in the Vale, and in few places elsewhere, was the taste for the picturesque more remarkably expressed than at Hestercombe. There, from the 1750s until his death in 1791, Coplestone Warre Bampfylde created a landscape garden in a high-sided combe behind the mansion, beautifying it with ponds, a temple, a mausoleum, a witch's house and a cascade. The cascade, recently brought back to life as part of a major programme of restoration, is no less arresting today than it was to Bampfylde's contemporaries. In 1787, the Second Viscount Palmerston described it as 'a most romantick and beautiful object from several parts of the ground, and ... on the whole one of the best things of the kind I have seen in the territory of any private person'.

None of the later mansions and grounds created locally during the 19th century could quite achieve the evocative power of Hestercombe or the serenity of Hatch Court, but there was often no lack of architectural ambition. High on the Blackdowns at Otterford, for example, William Beadon of Taunton built the mansion called Otterhead House in 1841 (demolished 1947), surrounding it with landscaped grounds incorporating a series of lakes; and at Norton Fitzwarren in 1843 Norton Manor was lavishly constructed for Charles Noel Welman.

In towns and larger villages houses were also built, sometimes speculatively, which reflected the more modest aspirations of professional and middle-class families. The rebuilding in the late 18th century of many houses in Milverton, particularly in North Street, added Georgian elegance to a town where thatched cottages of 'rough stone or plaister'd mud walls' then predominated, and Wellington by the 1780s had already acquired many of the 'good brick houses' which survive in the High Street today.

The greatest changes, as usual, took place in Taunton. There, in addition to the building of several fine individual houses such as Mansfield House and Mary Street House, some major civic, institutional and residential developments took place. At the very heart of the town in 1772, the inns, medieval Guildhall and other buildings which crowded on Taunton's Cornhill were replaced by a brick-built Market House designed by the versatile Mr. Bampfylde of Hestercombe. The Market House, which still dominates the town today,

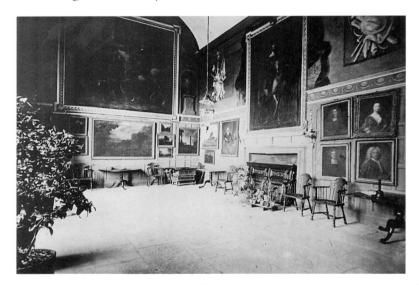

113 The Great Hall at Hestercombe, *c*.1873, shortly before its contents were dispersed and the house was remodelled by the Portman family.

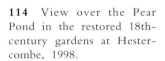

114 View over the Pear Pond in the restored 18th-century gardens at Hestercombe, 1998.

115   The Market House, the Parade and the New Market, Taunton, copied by Harry Frier from an illustration of 1829 by Edward Turle.

116   The Parade, Taunton, *c.*1850.

originally included two flanking arcades to accommodate market traders, an assembly room where the young Franz Liszt played the piano in 1840, and other rooms intended for 'the purposes of justice, amusement and pleasure'. An architecturally ambitious hospital was also begun in 1772 on rising ground south of Silver Street. But the building—later a Franciscan convent and now part of King's College—failed to attract funds for its completion, and not until 1812 did the Taunton and Somerset Hospital open on a new site in East Reach.

Perhaps the simplest but most strikingly successful development in Georgian Taunton was Hammet Street, begun in 1788. It paid its tribute to the Middle Ages by opening a splendid vista towards the tower of St Mary's Church, and provided much-needed

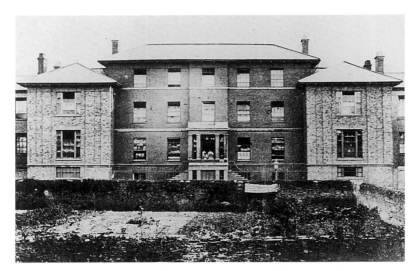

117 The Taunton and Somerset Hospital, *c.*1865.

118 Hammet Street and the church of St Mary Magdalene, Taunton, *c.*1791.

accommodation for 'genteel families out of trade'. The creation of the street was promoted, partly for political reasons, by Sir Benjamin Hammet (d.1800), M.P. for the town, who was also responsible for rescuing Taunton Castle from decay and so ensured that the Assize courts continued to meet there. The first half of the 19th century was to witness much other development in Taunton, including the imposing New Market House of 1821-2. But the physical creation of the Georgian town was largely completed with the building of an elegant red-brick street called the Crescent, begun to the west of the town centre in 1807.

119 The Masonic Hall and the Crescent, Taunton, 1942. The Masonic Hall was built as a Catholic chapel in 1822, a purpose it fulfilled until St George's Church was opened in 1860.

JUST AS the ambitious Georgian houses of Taunton Deane reflected an affluent gentry and a rising middle class, so the condition of local churches and chapels was an index of the more varied fortunes of the Vale's religious life. In an age not remarkable for piety, only the nonconformists continued to flourish locally during the 18th century. They supported the Taunton Academy where, for 30 years, Henry Grove (1684-1738), the friend of Isaac Watts, gave instruction to young men intended for the nonconformist ministry; they continued to attend nonconformist meetings in great numbers; and they lavished money on building or rebuilding their chapels. Paul's Meeting in Taunton remained the Vale's chief centre of Presbyterian or Independent worship through-

out the 18th century, and in 1798 the chapel was rebuilt largely in its present form. Presbyterian chapels also rose at Wiveliscombe in 1708, and at Bishops Hull in 1718, while at Wellington a Presbyterian chapel of 1730 was joined the following year by a new chapel for the town's Baptist congregation. In Mary Street, Taunton, a Baptist (later Unitarian) chapel was established by 1691 and rebuilt in 1721, its splendid oak fittings including the pulpit from which Coleridge often preached during 1797-8. The Quakers acquired a permanent home in Bath Place, Taunton, in 1693, and another in the High Street at Wellington the following year. Methodism reached the district through the efforts of John Wesley himself during a series of visits made between 1743 and 1789. The

120 Interior of Mary Street Unitarian Chapel as rebuilt in 1721.

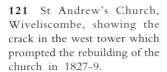

121 St Andrew's Church, Wiveliscombe, showing the crack in the west tower which prompted the rebuilding of the church in 1827-9.

former Octagon Chapel in Middle Street, Taunton, was built in 1776 at Wesley's instigation, and nine years later he was on hand to open Wellington's first Methodist chapel in Burman's Lane. His presence in Taunton Deane was frequently controversial. In 1743 he was heckled when he preached at Taunton's Market Cross, and after addressing a crowd at Hillfarrance in 1750 he noted in his journal that 'Three or four boors would have been rude if they durst but the odds against them was too great'.

While nonconformist chapels and congregations thrived, often counting wealthy tradesmen and professional people among their supporters, the Anglican churches of the district suffered a long neglect. Many incumbents during the 18th and early 19th centuries were absentees or pluralists who left their churches in the care of ill-paid curates; services in rural parishes were generally infrequent and poorly attended; and lack of money had reduced the fabric of many churches to a perilous condition.

At Creech St Michael in the 1780s the plaster was 'crumbling down daily' from mould-covered walls; St Giles's Church at Bradford on Tone was 'going fast to decay'; and at St Andrew's Church in Wiveliscombe the structure was failing so badly that the pillars of the south aisle were more than a foot out of perpendicular. At least a few parish churches benefited from the gifts of wealthy donors. St Mary's Church at Bishops Lydeard, for example, was given a fine new organ in 1751 and also acquired a baroque altar piece 22 feet high. This remarkable structure, topped by '3 large urns embelishd with cherubs, festoons etc', was rivalled by other vanished altar pieces at Wellington and Wilton, the latter given by the munificent Sir Benjamin Hammet. But less fortunate churches, especially those which were small or remote, merely decayed, so that by the 1830s Curland church was far from unique in having become 'a damp, dirty, and filthy building, fit for a pig's stye'.

The restoration of the Vale's parish churches waited for the 19th-century revival of Anglicanism itself, and for the emergence of social and religious attitudes which no longer tolerated west gallery musicians, neglectful clergy and dilapidated buildings. By the 1840s, incumbents were less often absentees from their parishes, and men such as the uproarious hunting vicar of Creech St Michael, Henry Cresswell (1787-1849), were giving way to clergy of more sober habits and antiquarian interests. James Cottle, vicar of St Mary's in Taunton, directed a major restoration of his church in 1843-4, and in the course of the next 30 years there were few churches in the Vale which were not either enlarged, drastically restored or entirely rebuilt. Restoration at Corfe in 1844 and 1858, for example, replaced nearly all the ancient fabric with a building in the neo-Norman style; at West Hatch in 1861 the church was reconstructed from the ground up as an

122 Gallery in St Michael's Church, Creech St Michael, c.1905. The gallery, which is evidently 18th century, formerly stood at the entrance to the chancel where Edmund Rack saw it in about 1785.

123 View of Taunton from St George's Church, *c.*1870, showing the tower of St James's Church in the course of being rebuilt.

enlarged version of the original building; and at West Monkton five years later an array of box pews failed, as usual, to survive the hand of the restorers. Even the great west towers of St Mary's and St James's in Taunton finally succumbed. Both were taken down and rebuilt in facsimile, the first reaching completion in 1862, the second (slightly modified) in 1875. Much of the work undertaken by the Victorian restorers was long overdue and left the churches of Taunton Deane in better repair than at any time since the late Middle Ages.

But there must be cause, nonetheless, to regret the chancel screens which were thoughtlessly destroyed (as at Bradford on Tone, Creech St Michael, Orchard Portman, Wellington and West Buckland), the medieval plaster that was hacked from walls, and the box pews and benches which vanished forever. By the 1870s, Georgian neglect of the Vale's parish churches and Victorian zeal in restoring them had together resulted in artistic destruction unmatched in its scale since the Reformation.

7

The Golden Vale

'ARAINY STORMY MORNING', noted William Marshall, the agricultural writer, as he set out from Taunton in September 1794. 'How convenient is a carriage, and how productive of information! A tablet full of interesting facts in travelling five or six miles.' He went south on the turnpike road through Ruishton and Thornfalcon, recording what he saw in a 'rich fine country' of mistletoe growing in the orchards and wheat stubbles ploughed under after harvest. He commended some promising turnips and good young cattle, took note also of the many ox-carts along his way and the labourers at work with the pointed shovels peculiar to the West Country. At the lime kilns wagons stood ready to carry lime for the newly-ploughed fields, and on every side elm trees grew in the hedgerows. There seemed nothing, on the brink of the 19th century, to mar the fame of the 'Golden Vale'.

The farming landscape described by Marshall had in many respects changed hardly at all during the course of more than a century. Immediately surrounding Taunton the bishop of Winchester's lands were still held as virtual freeholds by his manorial tenants; the greater gentry continued to own major estates, mostly at a little distance from the town; and an array of other freeholders and leaseholders filled the remaining agricultural land. Important changes had nevertheless been taking place. On the bishopric estates, many of the small yeoman farms of the 16th and 17th centuries had been passing into the hands of outsiders, either by inheritance or purchase, so that those who worked the land and those who owned it were increasingly distinct. At the same time farms throughout the Vale were being amalgamated as never before. At Norton Fitzwarren in the 1780s Isaac Welman and William Hawker, lords of the manor, promoted the creation of larger farms by refusing to renew long leases on small and inefficient holdings. By the 1830s, Edward Berkeley Portman was

124 Remains of a 19th-century lime kiln in Thurlbear Wood. The kiln was supplied by blue lias quarries at the edge of the wood and was one of the many kilns which existed in the area from the Middle Ages onwards. The last of the local limeburners, Tom Burt, operated kilns for George Small and Sons until the outbreak of the Second World War.

125 Edward Berkeley Portman (1799-1888) by Sir George Hayter, 1833. E.B. Portman was created Baron Portman in 1837 and 1st Viscount in 1873.

vigorously pursuing the same policy. He amalgamated tenant farms whenever he could and provided fine new farmhouses and barns for carefully selected tenants. He was also responsible for creating major new areas of farmland when, in 1833, the enclosure of Neroche Forest was finally achieved. Though many farms continued to be of less than one hundred acres throughout the 19th century, the steady process of amalgamation and expansion meant that others of two or even three hundred acres also became common.

Dairying and animal husbandry remained major elements in the farming economy of Taunton Deane during the late 18th century. North Devon cattle and Dorset sheep were kept in profusion, and farmers who held land on the Vale's surrounding hills were often specialists in stock raising. At Otterford in the 1780s, for example, 'great numbers of young cattle' were being reared and then sent into the moors for fattening. William Marshall nonetheless concluded that Taunton Deane at this

period was 'properly an arable district', and when, on one of his visits in the 1790s, he looked out over the Vale from high ground, he estimated that half the land which lay before him was being used to grow crops. Fifty years later, little had changed: in the period 1837-42, 50 per cent of the Vale was arable land, while 41 per cent was given over to pasture, meadow and orchards. Wheat and barley were, as ever, the chief arable crops, though there were smaller quantities of oats, roots, peas and beans. The farming landscape also contained the more vivid accents of some local specialities. Flax was for a time widely grown, and at Bishops Hull in the 1780s the flax crop was commended by Edmund Rack for its 'very beautiful appearance'; at Orchard Portman in 1820, 20 acres of hop gardens were planted which survived until about 1845; and on the lias clay around Hatch Beauchamp and Staple Fitzpaine extensive crops of teasels, intended for cloth-finishing in the northern textile industry, could be found later in the 19th century.

But to locals and visitors alike nothing was more characteristic of Taunton Deane than its celebrated apple orchards. Cider apples such as the Cockagee, the Golden Pippen, the Red Streak, the Royal Wilding and the White Sour were grown throughout the district in the 1780s, and by 1837-42 almost five per cent of Taunton Deane was covered with orchards. Stoke St Mary was said to be producing 'some of the best cider in the kingdom' in 1833; at Heathfield the Revd Thomas Cornish (d.1856) planted orchards from which cider of 'champagne quality' was soon being made; and at Kingston St Mary the emergence by 1830 of the Kingston Black, a cider apple which did not require blending with other varieties, ensured for the parish a long-lasting West Country fame.

Progressive farming methods were occasionally to be found in this land of plenty, especially on some of the gentry estates. At Ruishton in about 1775, Robert Procter Anderdon of Henlade House became one of the first West Country landowners to use a seed drill. At Bishops Lydeard in 1813, John Winter of Watts House had recently installed a water-powered threshing machine—possibly in response to the labour shortage caused by the Napoleonic Wars—and by the 1850s water wheels for driving farm machinery could also be found on the Esdaile estate at Cothelstone and the Portman estate at Orchard Portman. But despite such innovations, agriculture in Taunton Deane was chiefly remarkable for conservatism. Edmund Rack thought local farmers owed more to the richness of their land than to agricultural skill, and criticised their unwillingness to try new methods such as the growing of turnips for animal fodder. The distinctive reddish-brown oxen of Taunton Deane continued to draw 'ploughs of the rudest pattern' well into the 19th century, and plough teams of eight or ten oxen were in regular use

at Cutliffe Farm, Wilton, as late as the 1860s. By that time the steam plough could also be heard 'panting and breathing hard in the early morn' on some farms in the district. But when, in 1875, the Royal Agricultural Society brought its show to Taunton, machines had not ceased to be objects to gaze on with wonder.

THE EVIDENT PROSPERITY of Taunton Deane in the late 18th and early 19th centuries only partly concealed a growing crisis of poverty for labouring families. A series of poor harvests in the 1790s, and the economic consequences of war with France, sent grain prices to unprecedented levels, and in 1801 the proclamation was read in local churches 'for frugality in the use of every species of grain'. By the end of the Napoleonic Wars in 1815, many farm labourers had been thrown into partial dependence on the poor rates, so

126 'Cutting a heavy piece of clover' at Wilcox Farm, Hatch Beauchamp, 1906. 'The four men standing were all over 70 and they were very good hands especially with scythes and could drink as much cider as any four men in Somerset.'

that the distinction between labourers and paupers began to vanish altogether. At the same time the population of the Vale was increasing more rapidly than ever before. Between 1801 and 1831 it rose by 35 per cent from almost 27,000 to almost 36,500 (based on figures for the borough of Taunton and the hundreds of Taunton Deane, Kingsbury West, and Milverton). Taunton itself experienced an enormous 52 per cent increase from 5,794 to 11,139. In the face of such transforming change old systems of poor relief began to break down and costs rose alarmingly. In the parish of Pitminster, for example, the annual cost of poor relief rose from an average of £433 in 1783-5 to £1,549 in 1813.

The rural hardship which had lasted more than a generation reached its climax early in the 1830s. At the end of 1829 severe weather left hundreds of labourers around Taunton without employment and without food, such that Mr. W. Davis, a resident of the town, could write, 'Our houses have repeatedly been besieged by large bodies of men ... sometimes 40 or 50 in a company, soliciting relief for themselves and their starving families.. By June 1830, news had reached the town of incendiarism at Bridport and, in the months which followed, rick burning and machine breaking throughout the southern counties marked the progress of the century's worst agricultural disturbances. When the government asked why

127   Richard (Dicky) Wilmot, 'a Taunton character', in about 1865. The caption to the photograph records that he was born at Musgrove Farm, Wilton, and died in an outbuilding at Osborne House. He was the only child of prosperous parents.

128   The west end of St Michael's Church, Milverton, including benefaction boards describing charities for the poor endowed by Richard Westcombe of Oake and John Weekes of Nynehead. The weekly distribution of money by overseers to the deserving poor often took place in churches or churchyards.

129 Taunton Union Workhouse, *c.*1865. The building was completed in 1838 and followed one of the model designs of the architect Sampson Kempthorne.

such events should have happened, from Bishops Hull came the answer, 'the wretchedness of the labouring classes', and from North Curry, 'revenge of many, whose ancestors, or themselves, have been renters of small farms, which are now thrown into large ones, and which consolidation has rendered them beggars and labourers'. In the event, no one in the Vale expressed a sense of grievance in 'tumultory meetings and diabolical acts'. But Edward Esdaile of Cothelstone did recall that 'a visible discontent pervaded the lower classes'.

The government's response to the needs of the poor was the creation of union workhouses under the Poor Law Amendment Act of 1834. Parish-based workhouses had long played a limited part in local relief: in 1776 they ranged in size from the workhouse at Wellington, containing 150 inmates, to its tiny counterpart at Oake, which contained only four. The new legislation deprived parishes of their long-established independence as units of relief and grouped them into unions which

shared a common workhouse. The unions based on Taunton and Wellington, together covering the whole of Taunton Deane, were created in 1836, and it was some reflection of the harsh regime which was soon imposed that within two years the costs of relief in the Taunton union had fallen by 30 per cent. The Rev. Henry Barker of Haydon House gave local expression to the views of the Poor Law reformers. In 1834 he wrote:

> We want above all things to excite a spirit of exertion which bears up against petty misfortune, and enables the poor to prove the truth of the maxim, that 'the relief which comes from themselves, is the best and most effectual'.

A correspondent to the *Taunton Courier* 10 years later saw matters differently. 'Proper and fair wages for a fair day's work' were what poor labourers most required, an opinion echoed by rioters at Taunton in 1847 who demanded that market traders should lower their prices.

NOT ALL WAS HARDSHIP for the labouring classes, not even at the worst of times. 'Monkton for rich, Cheddon for poor, Kingston for thieves, Lydeard for whores' went the local rhyme, neatly expressing the fact that parishes, or small groups of them, were kingdoms unto themselves, always distinct in character and prosperity. Accidents of the soil had some bearing in matters of prosperity, but perhaps most important was the ability or willingness of landlords to encourage good methods among their farm tenants and to provide good cottages for the farm labourers. The Portman family, on their great estate within Taunton Deane, left an honourable legacy of good labourers' cottages. 'Mr Portman took me to see one of Lord Portman's model cottages', wrote a government official at Staple Fitzpaine in 1869. 'Very neat, built of stone and slate, two rooms below with a vestibule and three bedrooms above.' At Hillfarrance that same year, however, the cottages were described as in general 'very bad', a reflection of the poverty or negligence of the parish's numerous small landowners; and at Wiveliscombe,

Mr. Lucas, the schoolmaster, described a group of three labourers' cottages, each with one bedroom, which had until recently sheltered a total of 27 people.

Whether they lived in comfort or in squalor, the life of toil for most farm labourers began at an early age. James Hoare, whose father farmed 20 acres at Staple Fitzpaine in the 1860s, was seven years old when he began work driving his father's plough. His village contemporary, Alfred Dinham, was only a year older when he also became a plough boy, receiving at first 3d. a day with a pint of cider and graduating by the age of 13 to 6d. a day with 1½ pints:

> Horses knocked me down once, but found I could manage them ... Made a boy terrible tired walking about with the horses. Had supper when I came in, taties sometimes, sometimes bread and cheese, no meat except on Sundays.

Other village children, before taking regular work, were often set to 'mazing', or keeping pigs, in the autumn months, and bird-scaring in the spring, the latter a task in which

130 Frederick and Eliza Vile with their family at Church Farm, Thurlbear, c.1895. Mr. Vile was a tenant of Lord Portman's and worked on the Portman estate.

131 Pupils at Hatch Beauchamp school, *c*.1905. The child in the front row appears to be wearing his best suit of clothes for the occasion, to his evident disgust.

girls were well represented. On Mr. Hancock's large farm at Halse the bird scarers would make a hut for themselves when it rained and some-times light a fire against the cold, while across the fields they sang out the rhyme, 'Get away Jack carrion crow, Why do you use your master so?' For most girls in the 1860s, the minor agricultural occupations of their early years, together with the back-breaking demands of glove-sewing, generally gave way at about the age of 13 to domestic service in a big house or the town. For boys, unless they learnt a trade or took up a local speciality such as lime burning, the routines of the farming year fixed the boundaries of their world from childhood on. Only their wages made a change for the better as adult life began: 7s. a week, with a daily allowance of three pints of cider, was reckoned to be the labourer's average wage in the Taunton area in 1850; 20 years later 9s. a week was not uncommon.

FORMAL EDUCATION played an increasing part in the lives of 19th-century village children, and in some of the Vale's rural communities already had a long history. Parish schools, such as the school being kept by the parish clerk of Trull in 1623, were relatively common in the 17th century, and by the 18th century money to found charity schools was being given by local benefactors. Endowments for schools at Kingston St Mary (1720), Oake (1722), Ruishton (1742), Trull (1756), Cheddon Fitzpaine (1756) and Otterford (1769) marked stages in the slow process by which the children of the labouring poor acquired larger expectations of the world, though seldom more than a modest degree of learning. By 1818 a large number of day and Sunday schools existed locally, the latter intended chiefly for the education of poor children who worked during the week. At Combe Florey in 1818 the rector's daughters helped to run a Sunday school attended by thirty or forty children. At Kingston, the Sunday school, attended by all the poor children of the parish, was elaborately staffed by a headmaster and his wife, two under masters and several monitors. And at Pitminster some seventy children were served by 'three or four reading schools' as well as a school which taught writing and accounts.

Only slowly, however, did piecemeal efforts to educate the poor give way to the establishment of large numbers of more permanent schools, both in the country and

the town. The Original Infants School was opened in Mary Street, Taunton, in 1828 and, three years later, the Central Schools were built in Church Square. Thereafter, elementary schools appeared throughout the Vale, many of them supported by the voluntary contributions of mainly Anglican congregations as well as by the National Society. By 1870, when the government at last undertook to provide free elementary education for those too poor to pay, hardly a child in Taunton Deane lived more than a short distance from a permanently established school.

132   Pupils at North Town Council Schools, Taunton, celebrating Empire Day in 1909. The opening of council schools for boys, girls and infants at North Town in 1907 reflected the growing demand for elementary school places in Taunton at the beginning of the 20th century.

RURAL COMMUNITIES were also experiencing less welcome changes at this period. 'There is a great migration going on', F.B. Portman, the rector of Staple Fitzpaine, wrote in 1869. 'The people go like a flock of sheep; one member of a family finds himself thriving elsewhere and writes home to say so, and the rest follow.' Others, too, read the symptoms of profound change. 'I was struck with the scarcity of young men and maidens', an anonymous traveller through the district noted in 1863. 'A fair average, perhaps, of children, but no corresponding proportion of manhood and young women. The labourers seemed to me generally to be old screws, and the women fit partners for them.' Those who sought reasons for what they found ascribed much to the advent of farm machinery and to the opportunities for work offered by towns such as Weston and Taunton. As the century wore on into a period of great agricultural depression, caused chiefly by an influx of foreign grain, few doubted any longer that the town, not the country, was the place to thrive.

133 James Lovell of Broomfield, photographed by the folk song collector Cecil Sharp in the summer of 1908. James Lovell sang numerous songs for Sharp, including 'John Barleycorn', 'All Jolly Fellows that Follow the Plough', 'The Saucy Sailor' and 'The Constant Farmer's Son'.

VISITORS TO TAUNTON during the 19th century seldom failed to be impressed by the town's prosperity as a marketing centre, as well as by its broad, well-paved streets, elegant town houses, and ambitious public buildings. The efforts of the improvers, from the mid-18th century onward, had achieved a transformation. But change had not come easily. For at least the first half of the 19th century the lawlessness of Taunton's poorer suburbs—including East Reach, Wilton, North Town and Tangier—together with the sewage stench of open drains, were among many reminders of a less comfortable reality.

Taunton's efforts to improve itself during the late Georgian and early Victorian periods were hampered especially by the divided state of its local government. The town's charter, restrictively renewed in 1677, gave Taunton a corporation which included a mayor, two aldermen and 21 other burgesses. A failure to fill up vacancies, however, caused the charter to lapse in 1792, and despite periodic agitation by the people of Taunton it was not until 1877 that a new charter was finally granted. During that long interim, the government of the town was in part carried on by officials of the bishop of Winchester's borough court leet. But their power had long been in decline and ebbed yet further when, in 1822, Bishop Tomline severed the Winchester link altogether. After more than 900 years he sold Winchester's rights in the manor and the borough to Thomas Southwood of Pitminster, retaining only a claim to 'mines and minerals'.

Real power lay with the county justices—supported from 1839 by an inadequate borough police force—as well as with the trustees of Taunton Market. The trustees came into existence in 1768, when the first of Taunton's

134   Taunton Police Force in 1885.

135   The surviving part of the former Wilton Gaol, now incorporated into Taunton police station. A house of correction, or bridewell, replacing a predecessor near the town bridge, was built on the site in 1754 and was successively enlarged. It became the county gaol in 1843 and was closed as a civil prison in 1884. The building on the right was the gaol's infirmary.

Market Acts was passed, and until the middle of the 19th century they remained effective masters of the town. The Market Acts not only permitted the trustees to build the Market House, but gave them powers to regulate the markets, clean and light the streets, construct sewers and lay water pipes. They provided gas lighting for the town's principal streets following the formation of a gas company in 1821 and employed scavengers to keep the streets swept and weeded; but the drainage needs of the growing town quite soon defeated them.

In 1821 James Lackington Rice privately undertook to provide sewers for the central area of Taunton, with an outlet discharging into the River Tone. Lackington's sewers were poorly designed and when the river was high caused sewage to back up into cellars. But the town's longer-established open drains were far worse. In 1847, the Church Square drain, which ran behind North Street, was said to contain 'four or five feet of solid privy soil', and so foul was the stench rising from it that Mr. Cottle, vicar of St Mary's, could scarcely walk in his garden when the wind came from the west. The town's many courts or 'colleges' were especially unhealthy. The colleges each contained ten to twenty close-packed houses— originally built to swell the numbers in the borough eligible to vote at Parliamentary elections—and were drained into foul open cesspits which contaminated the wells: Collier's Court in East Street had an open cesspit ten feet wide and six feet deep. It was little wonder that infant mortality in the town was significantly higher than in the countryside around it, or that fevers, dysentery and smallpox were all occasional visitors.

In September 1849, despite opposition from the Market Trustees, Taunton took advantage of new legislation and acquired its own Local Board of Health. Almost at once the modernisation of the town's drainage system began, a process which was largely completed in 1877 when Taunton's Urban Sanitary Authority, formed five years earlier, opened a new sewage works at Lambrook. Despite the inadequacies of the Lambrook works, their completion meant that never again would 'noxious effluvia', reported in 1847, be a daily offence to large numbers of inhabitants or pose so grave a threat to their health.

Taunton's water supply was also transformed during these years. In the 1840s pumps and wells supplied water copiously, but of a quality so hard that it was of little use for domestic purposes. The River Tone and the increasingly polluted streams that entered it provided an even more inadequate source, and left many people with little choice but to buy in water from those possessing rainwater tanks. Taunton waited until 1858 before it acquired its own Water Works Company, and the following year water piped along an eight-inch main finally reached the town from springs above Angersleigh. The supply was at first intermittent. But when, in 1879, the Local Board of Health built a reservoir at Blagdon, clean water became permanently available to most of Taunton's inhabitants, and the town's insanitary past could at last begin to be forgotten.

136 View behind 44 and 45 East Street, Taunton, by Evacustes A. Phipson, 1909.

TAUNTON'S CHARACTER as a place of trade changed greatly during the later Georgian and Victorian periods. In the 1780s, the woollen cloth industry still employed significant numbers both in the town and the villages around it. Poor spinners at Creech St Michael, Kingston and West Monkton were supplying the Taunton looms in that period, and manufacturers in Wilton and Bishops Hull were producing serges, druggets and duroys. But the Taunton industry was already far advanced in decline, and Joshua Toulmin in 1791 reported that houses in the town's suburbs, formerly occupied by cloth workers, were now in ruins.

Changing tastes, falling prices, and the introduction of spinning machines by north country manufacturers partly explained the

137 Tonedale, Wellington, *c.*1950. Tonedale was created as a woollen factory by Thomas Fox between 1801 and 1803, and was soon employing 3,600 workers. It was destroyed by fire in 1821 but quickly rebuilt.

town's rapid eclipse. Popular opinion also blamed the disastrous effects of contested Parliamentary elections, especially the Taunton by-election of 1754. John Halliday, one of the members for the town, died in June that year, and for the next six months there followed a campaign marked by lavish entertainment in inns and alehouses, and by mob violence which cost several lives. Demand for cloth was high, but 'through the idleness and debauchery of the season' cloth merchants were sent away empty-handed and looked to other towns to supply them. Wellington was one beneficiary of Taunton's misfortune, and by the end of the 18th century the Fox and Elworthy families had established Wellington among the West Country's major cloth producers. Wiveliscombe's cloth trade also prospered. It supplied baize to line soldiers' coats and serge to clothe West Indian slaves, only entering a final decline when in 1833 the abolition of slavery throughout the colonies deprived the town of its chief market.

For some who had depended on Taunton's woollen cloth industry, silk manufacture, introduced to the town in 1778, provided an alternative livelihood. A silk-throwing mill, with water-powered machinery, was built in Upper High Street in 1781, and shortly afterwards other premises were opened

in Canon Street. By 1822, 1,000 looms in and near the town, together with silk-throwing mills in Taunton, Staplegrove and Preston Bowyer, were said to be employing about 1,800 people. Four years later, when the threat of foreign imports marked the beginning of recession, the *Taunton Courier* thought there were 4,400 local silk workers, though that was probably an over-estimate. The Taunton trade was languishing by 1828, and never again did it thrive as in the previous 30 years. But diversification, first into lace manufacture and gloving, then into collar and shirt making, ensured long-term survival for the Taunton textile industry: by 1888, there were said to be nearly 1,500 collar workers employed in the town, a number which increased considerably when, in 1891 and 1899, Henry Van Trump opened new factories. Other industries also flourished. By 1849 they included iron and brass foundries, three breweries, a tannery, a fellmongery, and two dye works. Nine steam engines were at work in the town that year, and together were producing a total of 71 horse power.

Throughout the rapid changes of the 19th century, Taunton's markets and fairs provided strong links of continuity with the past. The markets, in particular, flourished as never before, not least because the restrictive powers of the Market Trustees prevented competition. In Wellington, by the 1880s, the rise of independent shopkeepers had reduced Wellington market to relative insignificance. But shopkeepers found it far harder to succeed in Taunton because the Market Act of 1768 forbade the independent sale of provisions or livestock within 1,000 yards of the market place. In response to widespread discontent, the Trustees became increasingly liberal in granting licences for shops to be set up, and by 1888 three butcher's shops and three fishmongers had been licensed within the 1,000-yard limit, as well as 10 grocers, 54 greengrocers, and nine corn merchants.

By the late 18th century, a market held on Wednesdays supplemented the town's long-established Saturday market, and some trade also continued on 'off-days' throughout the week. The Parade and the Market House arcades at first provided the main trading area. But butchers' stalls, together with those of other traders, were moved to the New Market House in 1822, and in 1868 a Corn Exchange, converted from the former Fish Market, was opened next to Castle Bow. Castle Green, from 1788, was home to the town's 'Great Market', where cattle, sheep and horses were traded on one Saturday a month (and later fortnightly). Complaints that the Great Market regularly

138   The Parade, Taunton, on a market day in the late 19th century. The Kinglake Cross was built in 1867 and dismantled in 1934.

139 & 140   *Above*. The livestock market on Castle Green, *c.*1880. *Below*. The market in 1901.

141 St Augustine Street, Taunton, *c*.1905. The building of the street formed part of the development of the Priory area of the town, begun in 1898.

blocked a main route into Taunton prompted short-lived moves to sites in East Reach and elsewhere. But none of the alternatives was popular, and not until 1929—three years after the Trustees gave up their powers to Taunton Borough Council—was the market provided with a new home in Priory Bridge Road.

The sale of cattle and horses also remained the staple trade of Taunton's two ancient fairs, one held in the centre of the town on 17 June, the other at North Town on 7 July. The respectable element of Victorian Taunton regarded both fairs as nuisances which encouraged bad behaviour and left the streets filthy for days afterwards. But an attempt to abolish the fairs in 1882 was unsuccessful, and not until the early years of the new century did they finally vanish.

TAUNTON INCREASED its borders rapidly during the Victorian period, chiefly to accommodate a growing population of working-class families. In 1840 'almost a new town' was taking shape in the Trinity area, and by 1844 speculative builders were so active locally that workmen came from afar to supply the necessary labour force. Other houses rose north of the river, chiefly from the 1870s onward, to ease the accommodation crisis of a town grown decidedly 'too big for its clothes'. Speculative builders also met the needs of monied and gentry families who, at the beginning of the Victorian era, complained that Taunton lacked not only a supply of suitable housing but a good public school where their sons could be educated. By 1861, 'handsome houses, with lawns and gardens, stables and

142 High-Victorian furnishings in a room at Wilton House, Taunton, *c*.1890. Wilton House was built in the late 18th century by Sir Benjamin Hammet.

143   The Wesleyan Collegiate Institution (later Queen's College), Taunton, in 1860.

coach-houses' were said to be rising at nearly every approach to the town. 'Gentlemen of fortune' were taking up residence in them, and Taunton had acquired not just one public school but several.

A fee-paid education, based chiefly on the study of Latin and Greek, had long been available at Taunton's 16th-century Grammar School, later known as the College School. Its distinguished 18th-century master, James Upton (d.1749), had made it one of the largest and most respected of England's provincial schools. But by the 19th century its site was considered too small, its funding was inadequate, and its links to the Church of England caused deep resentment among the town's powerful nonconformists. In 1842 the master, William Crotch, was forced to admit that apart from a 'noble schoolroom' his school possessed 'no attractions' whatsoever.

Competitors were not slow to appear. The earliest was a school established at Fullands House in 1840 which survived for less than 50 years. More enduring was the Wesleyan Collegiate Institution (called Queen's College from 1888) which was established on 'strictly

Wesleyan principles' in 1843 and was intended, Mr. Crotch believed, to 'supersede and ruin the College School'. The building at Haines Hill which the school now occupies was opened in 1847, and in the same year the Independent College (a Congregational foundation called Taunton School from 1899) established its first home on Wellington Road. King's College, the youngest of Taunton's large public schools, came late to the town. It was founded by Canon Woodward in 1880 and took over premises which, a decade before, had been built as an impressive new home for the College School. A revival of fortunes for the College School had been sadly short-lived and, after retreating in 1877 to its original buildings at the centre of Taunton, it was finally wound up in 1885. Its influence did not, however, quite pass away. In 1890 its ancient endowment was transferred to a school known from that date as Bishop Fox's Girls' School. Together with Huish's Boys' School, founded in 1874, Bishop Fox's at last made available a secondary 'middle-class' education of the kind that prosperous farmers and successful tradesmen had long been seeking for their children.

THE PRIDE AND THANKFULNESS with which England marked Victoria's diamond jubilee in 1897 were fully shared by the people of Taunton. From the mayor and corporation a loyal address was sent to the Queen on behalf of the town. School children in their hundreds received jubilee medals and enjoyed celebration teas. And at a festival service in St Mary's Church, Prebendary Askwith betrayed only a hint of self-doubt when he described the jubilee as almost the fulfilment of English history:

> We stand, or we think we stand, where no foot of Englishman has ever been before, under the full noontide glare of England's proudest day, on the topmost height of our country's prosperity, in the unsullied sunshine of the Divine favour.

144 Alderman William Lock, with his wife, as mayor of Taunton in 1897, the year of Victoria's Diamond Jubilee.

145 Bridge Street, Taunton, decorated for Victoria's Diamond Jubilee in June 1897.

Though the pride was forgivable, the mood of that late-Victorian summer was destined to fade even before the outbreak of war in 1914. By 1912 the continued decay of farming communities left the Somerset writer, Edward Hutton, with a 'curiously solemn sense of having witnessed the passing of the old order', and those who had earlier left the countryside for the town were now in many cases searching at even greater distances for prosperity. A lecture given in the Assembly Rooms at Taunton in November 1910 was entitled 'Canada: its Opportunities and Possibilities', and by the end of the year the *Somerset County Gazette* was predicting for the spring an exodus from the district of farmers, farm labourers and domestic servants. Many duly booked passage with Hickman's of Bridgwater, local agents for the Canadian Pacific Railway, and left the shores of England forever with the promise of wages of four or five pounds a week. Such riches must have seemed almost irresistible at a time when rate-burdened local farmers were generally paying no more than 10s. a week with a cottage.

146   Fore Street and North Street, Taunton, *c.*1905, showing the town in its Edwardian high summer before the First World War. Taunton's tram service, from East Reach to the railway station, opened in 1901. It was extended to Rowbarton eight years later and closed in 1921.

147 Maypole dancing at a village fête, Hatch Beauchamp, 1907.

Those left behind in Taunton Deane remained faithful to accustomed patterns, and it was quietly appropriate that the village fêtes of a wet bank holiday coincided with the outbreak of war in August 1914. Within days a new Taunton Recruiting Committee had been formed, and Colonel Henry Patton, commander of the Second Volunteer Battalion of the Somerset Light Infantry, was greeted with cheers at a recruiting meeting in Vivary Park. In the weeks that followed he was to be found at Kingston St Mary, Creech St Michael, Hatch Beauchamp and Bickenhall, urging all eligible men to search their consciences with the question, 'What valid reason have I for not doing something in the greatest struggle of all time?' Thousands answered the call to action, and from the Borough of Taunton came no

fewer than 3,500 recruits. Only in the months ahead, as the Taunton papers began to report the names of casualties from the battlefields of France, was there a growing sense of the calamity war represented and the watershed it marked for local communities.

When peace came at last in 1918, it was not unexpected. The people of Taunton and the villages around it had been waiting for days when at 11 o'clock on 11 November they heard the signal that told them the Armistice was agreed. From the Electric Light Works in St James's Street the siren sounded 11 times across the Vale, and at Allen's Foundry the anvils were fired. Adults and children from surrounding villages converged on the town, joining those who 'from school, factory, work-shop, and business house' had already poured

148 The Corporals' Room at the Depot of the Somerset Light Infantry, Taunton, about the period of the First World War.

149 Nurses and patients at the military hospital established at Hatch Park, Hatch Beauchamp, 1916. At the centre sits Mrs. Gore-Langton, a member of the family which owned the house.

into the streets. The crowds laughed and sang and flags were everywhere. But even at the height of celebration the sight of 'many sad faces' was a reminder of terrible losses—losses which included 464 men from Taunton alone.

It was at about 9 o'clock that evening, after relative calm had settled on the streets of Taunton, that wounded soldiers gathered at a bonfire lit in front of the Red Cross Hospital. As children from neighbouring streets arrived to share in the fun, the men joined hands around the blaze and with a mixture of emotion which is not recorded brought the first day of peace to its close by singing 'Auld Lang Syne'.

8

Towards the Millennium

FOR THE FARMERS of Taunton Deane, the First World War marked a time of relative plenty after the long years of agricultural depression. The urgent need to increase home production ensured farming prosperity while the war continued. But that prosperity did not long survive the return to peace, and during the inter-war years local farmers, and more especially their farm labourers, often endured great hardship. Villages slumbered as the slow drift from the land continued; rents on the great Portman estate frequently went unpaid; and the routes that converged on Taunton were filled with those who had been reduced to the level of tramps, or 'roadsters'. A child on the way to school at Cheddon Fitzpaine in this period saw a man faint into the road while he stood in a dole queue. The explanation was simple: 'We were told it was because he was hungry.'

Poverty in Taunton and on its outskirts also became increasingly conspicuous. In the 1920s at Galmington blankets were loaned out at 6d. a time to help the community's 'very poor people' during cold weather, and newly established allotments were eagerly taken up

150 Charles Owen ploughing at Cheddon Fitzpaine, 1939. Plough horses were rapidly being replaced by tractors at that period.

151 Captain Matterson, left, with Sylvia Spooner and Sybil, Viscountess Portman, at a meet of the Taunton Vale Foxhounds, Curry Rivel, *c.*1935. Lady Portman married Edward Claud Berkeley, 5th Viscount Portman, in 1926. When he died in 1942, death duties forced the sale to the Crown of estates at Staple Fitzpaine, Thurlbear, Orchard Portman and elsewhere; other estates in Durston, Hatch Beauchamp and North Petherton had been sold in 1930.

as a means of producing additional food. Unemployment was reported in 1921 to be the cause of 'acute distress' in Taunton itself, and inspired numerous municipal construction schemes mainly intended to give work to ex-servicemen. Priory Bridge and Priory Bridge Road, completed in 1922, were both undertaken for that reason, and in the course of the next 10 years a variety of road-widening and house-building schemes offered further sources of much-needed employment.

It was not surprising that many Taunton people, familiar with the effects of poverty in their own lives, were enthusiastic supporters of the General Strike, called on behalf of the miners in May 1926. On Sunday 9 May striking railwaymen and their wives attended a special service at Rowbarton Congregational Church, and in the evening a mass demonstration in Jarvis's Field (from 1929 the site of Taunton Market) was judged to be 'the largest public gathering of its kind held in Taunton for a very long while'. At another large meeting a South Wales miner described to the crowd the privations of his life, and J.A. Sparks, Taunton's prospective Labour candidate, declared that the same working classes who had defended their country in 1914 were now at the mercy of those concerned only with 'dividends and profits'.

Despite the unemployment and frequent hardships endured by many people after 1918, the inter-war years were also marked by great material progress both in town and country. By 1934, Taunton Corporation, which had bought the town's Electric Light Company in 1892, and the Wellington District Electric Company were not only supplying the Vale's urban areas with electricity, but had brought supplies at least within reach of a large part of the rural population as well. Sewerage schemes existed for rural communities such as Pitminster, Hatch Beauchamp, Ruishton, Trull, Norton Fitzwarren, Bradford and Bishops Lydeard, and only in the provision of mains water to rural areas was progress significantly slower. Although by 1934 water from the Blackdowns and the Quantocks was being piped to villages such as Staple Fitzpaine, Hatch Beauchamp and Bishops Lydeard, other communities waited many more years before a mains water supply finally reached them.

Centuries of rural isolation were vanishing forever during this period. A villager remembered that at Lydeard St Lawrence before the First World War those who travelled from home were forced to choose between walking, cycling, driving a horse and trap or taking the train from Crowcombe station. During the inter-war years, however, mobility was transformed by the introduction of a frequent and much-valued bus service, an innovation which was parallelled in villages throughout the district. Cars also made an appearance. A car was first registered to a Taunton owner in 1903, and in the same period other cars were becoming objects of fascination in many rural communities. The people of Bradford on Tone before the First World War would stand at their doors merely to watch Mr. Langworthy, the postmaster, drive down the road; the Hon. Teddy Portman of Hestercombe could be seen travelling in the green and yellow Cadillac he acquired in 1905; and at Stoke St Mary Ernest Trepplin was the proud owner of a car which his chauffeur seemed as often to be pushing as driving. It would not be long before cars

became so numerous that they ceased to arouse any special curiosity: in August 1938 a traffic census on the A38 near Bradford on Tone counted a daily average of 4,408 motor vehicles using the road between six in the morning and ten at night; and on one August day in 1950 no fewer than 920 motor vehicles and 409 bicycles were counted in East Street, Taunton, during a single hour.

The greatly increased mobility of the Vale's rural inhabitants gave them ready access to the new amenities the town had to offer. Taunton's Borough Library was built in Corporation Street in 1905 with the generous help of Andrew Carnegie; the racecourse on the road to Corfe saw its first race in September 1927; and two years later the new swimming baths in St James's Street became immediately

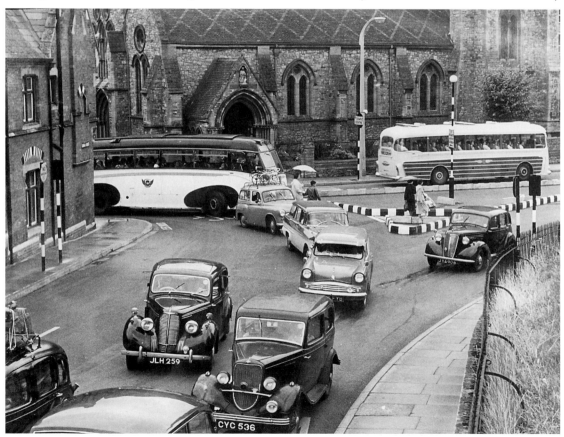

152   Taunton traffic at the junction of Park Street and Cann Street, 23 July 1960.

153   The Lyceum cinema, at the junction of Bridge Street and Station Road, Taunton *c*.1925. The site is now (1998) about to be redeveloped.

popular. But perhaps no attraction provided by the town was more widely enjoyed or more powerfully influential than the cinema. Taunton's first cinema was opened at the Corn Exchange in 1910. The Lyceum (1913), the Gaiety (1920) and the Gaumont Palace (1932) soon followed and, in addition to making the names of British and American film stars familiar to local people, brought news to them from the greater world. So too did the wireless broadcasts of the BBC, begun in 1922. When, on 3 September 1939, Eric Saffin and his family gathered round the wireless set in their home at Bishops Lydeard, the solemn announcement made by the Prime Minister, Neville Chamberlain, came as little surprise to them. 'My mother cried and my sister cried with her, without really knowing why. My father was angry ...' For the second time in a generation Britain was at war.

PREPARATIONS FOR WAR were already under way in Taunton Deane by the time Mr. Chamberlain spoke. Gas masks had been issued during the previous week throughout the Taunton ARP Area (which covered most of Taunton Deane); public air-raid shelters had been designated in churches and other buildings; and thousands of evacuees from London had started to arrive. By 4 September some 3,900 women, children and infants had been accommodated in Taunton and its surrounding villages, while the Wellington area received another 2,000. Most were readily welcomed, though some Taunton people at first defied the billeting officers and left evacuees 'waiting out in the street, wet through, many with babies in their arms'. In the first week after war was declared, Taunton drapers struggled to supply the call for black-out materials and grocers worked long hours to deal with orders from a population which had so suddenly increased in size. Quite soon, however, the people of Taunton Deane learned to cope with the many unfamiliar demands of wartime.

An invasion committee for the borough of Taunton had soon drawn up plans for resistance in the event of enemy attack and collected materials for building an emergency bridge over the river in case Tone Bridge were destroyed. In the balmy summer evenings of 1940 the newly created Home Guard (briefly called the Local Defence Volunteers) began training, armed at first with little more than some wooden rifles. Home Guard companies in rural parts of the Vale dragged tree branches into large, flat fields to prevent enemy gliders from landing, and by early August the Taunton platoons were learning to use Molotov cocktails in imminent expectation of a German assault.

They guarded the public utilities in and around Taunton as well as the concrete tank stops that appeared at every entrance to the town; and night by night they listened as enemy aircraft flew high above them. Though the Home Guard never did face the test of German invasion, the Battalion Commander in the Vale of Taunton, Lieut.-Col. Hilton Green, considered that by the end of 1941 his unlikely volunteer army had become a well-disciplined and well-armed force.

Lord Haw-Haw would sometimes cause alarm by showing an uncanny degree of local knowledge or by threatening the Vale with air raids. He referred on one occasion to a concert in the Victoria Rooms at Milverton which had taken place only a few days earlier, and in another broadcast commented that the Van Heusen's chimney in Taunton would serve as an excellent landmark. In the event, Taunton

154 ARP wardens at Taunton, *c*.1940.

Deane escaped major attacks, even though many high explosives and incendiary bombs were randomly dropped, chiefly over open country. The first bombs (some of the first in England as a whole) fell near the *Nag's Head*, Thornfalcon, on the night of 19-20 June 1940; just before daylight on 5 November a low-flying plane, probably aiming at a searchlight, machine-gunned the streets of Taunton; and on 28 June 1941 a large number of parachute mines came down in a wide arc around the town. One of them destroyed Wrantage school, and others landed at Stoke St Mary, Thurlbear, Churchstanton, Halse and Lydeard St Lawrence. Allied aircraft crashed in the countryside around Taunton on a number of occasions, often with loss of life; but perhaps longest remembered was the crash in March 1944 of an enemy Junkers Ju 88 on the drive to Hestercombe House. Three crew members survived, but the pilot was killed.

Far more significant than enemy action in making the war a reality for local people was the arrival of American soldiers in 1942. Though Pyrland Hall had been used since the early days of the war as headquarters of the British Army 8th Corps, the military presence in Taunton Deane had remained at a relatively low level. Now the rapid influx of American GIs altered everything. They took over nearly all military bases then existing around Taunton, including Burnshill Camp and Norton Manor Camp at Norton Fitzwarren and the vast stores complex called G50 which stood near by at Cross Keys. They established the 67th General Hospital at Musgrove Camp, the 101st in part of Norton Camp, the 185th at Sandhill Park, and 801st at Hestercombe House. The Hon. Constance Portman was determined to remain at Hestercombe after the arrival of her unexpected guests, and rather enjoyed their

155 One of the surviving warehouses forming part of the enormous stores depot called G50, now the Taunton Trading Estate. Bulldozers worked day and night for months to clear and level the ground for the depot which was served by a network of railway lines. G50 was the largest such complex in the whole south-western peninsula.

156 Hestercombe House, showing the celebrated gardens created by Sir Edwin Lutyens and Gertrude Jekyll. The gardens were commissioned by E.W.B. (Teddy) Portman in 1903. He would have succeeded to the viscountcy but for his early death in 1911. His widow, Constance, remained at Hestercombe until her own death in 1951.

presence in the house despite their taste for naked sunbathing in her beloved gardens.

US Military Police now appeared on the streets of Taunton to deal ruthlessly with disturbances involving American personnel; the American Services Club opened in the grounds of Flook House off Station Road; and in the skies overhead there appeared the unfamiliar sight of Dakotas, Flying Fortresses, Liberators and Mustangs. Soon the first black American troops arrived at Burnshill, and in their wake came an invasion of female camp followers from out of the county. They could be seen waiting at the camp gates day and night, and quickly set themselves up in local barns. Though Taunton people were shocked, white American soldiers were enraged. 'For the first time ever,' Eric Saffin remembers, 'I came into contact

with race hatred. It was something that we found hard to understand.'

As D-Day approached, a secret conference held at Shire Hall explained to local forces what they must do to assist the movement of American troops and to guard strategic sites. By mid-May 1944 convoys of lorries and tank transporters were appearing on every road, and finally, in the early hours of 6 June, the invasion began. From the aerodrome at Merryfield, Captain T.A. Bushell recalled, the massed squadrons of American troop carriers rose into the night sky.

> It was a truly spectacular sight. The sky over Taunton was temporarily filled with twinkling lights, for, in addition to the normal navigation lights of peace-time, each aircraft carried recognition lamps on the leading edge of the wings.

AMERICAN HOSPITAL.

CLOSING DOWN AT TAUNTON.

C.O.'s GRATITUDE TO TOWN.

THE opportunity of saying farewell and acknowledging with gratitude the hospitality shown them by the townspeople was taken by Col. R. B. Moore, officer in command of the 67th United States General Hospital, when he addressed Taunton Rotary Club at Moor's Cafe on Friday. Rotarian R. J. Case (president) presided.

Col. Moore said it was probably no longer a military secret that the 67th General Hospital had been at Taunton. As a matter of fact it was exactly 30 months ago that they came to the town, and he was glad of the opportunity of expressing the pleasure they had had in being there. Although they were disappointed at not being sent to a more active theatre of war he could not imagine a more delightful place to have been in than Taunton and the county of Somerset.

24,000 PATIENTS.

Col. Moore announced that his hospital closed at midnight the previous night and that during the 30 months it had been in operation had treated about 24,000 patients. Vouching for the fact that his personnel had enjoyed their association with the town, he mentioned that no fewer than 52 of the men had married British girls. Acknowledging the kindness and hospitality they had received, he said, "The memory of this place will always remain with us as the highlight of our war experience. I cannot begin to express for the members of my command what we owe you people. It is difficult to compare the treatment we have received here with what little the Americans have been able to do in America for the British. It seems to me that although you have had not nearly the resources and opportunities to do things because of your sufferings during the war, you have far outbalanced the ledger, and I am speaking not only for my own organisation but for every other military organisation that I have seen in England. It is probable we shall depart from here within a very few days and I shall have no opportunity of saying farewell personally to all the many friends I have made, but I think you, as representative citizens of Taunton, can convey to those of my acquaintance our heartfelt thanks for all you have done for us." (Applause).

Replying to a question, Col. Moore expressed the hope that their friends in Taunton would visit them in America, and said he hoped to come back and renew their acquaintance in a few years' time when conditions were normal.

Large numbers of American casualties from D-Day and after were brought in by train or flown to Merryfield and then taken by a 'vast fleet' of American military ambulances to the hospitals at Sandhill, Norton and Musgrove. Most of the wounded were returned to the United States as soon as they could travel, and the American presence in the area thus began to vanish almost as rapidly as it had appeared two years earlier. With the departure of the Americans, finally completed during 1945, one of the most remarkable and, in general, fondly remembered episodes in the whole history of Taunton Deane came to an end.

While the allies began to fight their way across Europe, Burnshill Camp at Norton Fitzwarren was taken over to house German prisoners of war. By late 1944, 1,600 Germans were held there, working during the day in the great stores depot, G50, under the supervision of American guards. The prisoners would reach the depot in a column several hundred strong; they 'marched smartly and sang as they marched'. By night they returned to a camp swept by searchlights and surrounded by watch-towers in which soldiers with machine guns were posted. The prisoners were well fed (possibly too well fed according to the local police) and received a cigarette and candy ration. Though they usually caused little trouble, it was reported that on two occasions 'SS elements' beat up prisoners who had been acting as stewards in the officers' mess and had passed on within the camp news overheard on the English radio. The Commandant, unable to identify those responsible for the beatings, deprived the whole camp of privileges for a fortnight.

Local celebrations for Victory in Europe, though falling short of the 'almost hysterical jubilation' reported from London, were never forgotten by those who witnessed them. At

157 Report from the *Somerset County Gazette*, 9 June 1945, of the closing down of the 67th United States General Hospital. It was taken over in 1946 to become Musgrove Park Hospital.

3 o'clock on VE Day, 8 May 1945, crowds gathered on Castle Green to hear Winston Churchill's victory broadcast, and the whistles of GWR engines at Taunton station sounded for fifteen minutes. By evening, bonfires were blazing out from local villages, and the town was a 'solid mass' of servicemen and civilians. They took part in impromptu street parties or joined the crowds at the centre of the town, where hundreds of people held hands and danced round and round the Market House, then formed a giant conga line that completely encircled the Parade. Eric Saffin remembered the evening as 'a spontaneous outburst of sheer joy'. On 9 May, a day of festivities in Vivary Park ended with hundreds dancing to the music of Ron Hancock and his Blue Bird Dance Band; and on Sunday 13 May a victory parade was watched by 'huge crowds' whose enthusiasm was only temporarily dampened by a sudden rainstorm.

For some, at least, the note of celebration seemed strained. The personal costs of war had once again been enormous, and the uncertainties of the future were greater even than in 1918. But none could doubt that war had been necessary: in the week before the people of Taunton Deane welcomed peace in Europe, a parliamentary delegation, including Taunton's MP, Lt.-Col. E.T.R. Wickham, brought back from Germany one of the first official reports of the concentration camps.

EVEN BEFORE THE WAR finally ended with the Japanese surrender on 14 August, Taunton, like Great Britain as a whole, was returning to peacetime concerns and peacetime politics. In the general election on 5 July, Col. Wickham was one of the many Conservative MPs swept away in the Labour landslide, and in his place the Taunton constituency chose Victor Collins, its first (and

158 Victor Collins, Labour MP for Taunton (second right), with (from left) Jack Humphrey, County Organiser of the National Union of Agricultural Workers, Earl Waldegrave, The Rt. Hon. Tom Williams, Minister of Agriculture and Fisheries, and Joe Gilling, County Chairman of the Somerset NFU, at the *County Hotel*, Taunton, 1948.

so far its only) Labour MP. When the result was announced outside the Municipal Buildings on 26 July, old Labour Party stalwarts were unable to restrain their tears, and Victor Collins, speaking with great emotion, described the day as 'one of the proudest and happiest, but at the same time one of the most solemn' of his life. At the Leycroft British Restaurant he told the crowd: 'It has been a marvellous day, not only in Taunton, but all over the country—perhaps the most important day any of us will see'; and at Wellington that evening, 2,000 supporters greeted him in pouring rain, then drew his car through the streets to Rockwell Green to the singing of 'For he's a jolly good fellow'.

The moment of triumph was short-lived. On 8 February 1950, three weeks before the general election held that year, Winston Churchill himself arrived in Taunton to rally support for Henry Hopkinson, the Conservative candidate. Churchill was given a tumultuous welcome in the streets of Taunton, and was greeted with 'great cheering' when he appeared on a balcony at the *County Hotel*. In a speech delivered in the Empire Hall, behind the hotel, he defended the Conservative record during the inter-war years, and then added, half humourously:

> Communism is a crime. Socialism a disease. It is a mental disease, but happily is not incurable. (Laughter). I hope Taunton will prepare a good dose, a really stiff dose, which, administered on February 23rd, may do a good deal to put many of our Socialist friends on the highroad to convalescence. (Laughter and applause).

That night at Taunton station the wheel-tapper, Percy Pinn, watched as the great man first settled himself in his carriage and then, with a look of quiet satisfaction, put on a pair of monogrammed slippers. On election day, though the Labour government survived, Hopkinson duly defeated Collins by 20,724 votes to 19,352.

159 Winston Churchill at the Empire Hall, Taunton, 8 February 1950. In the foreground is Geoffrey Farrant, President of Taunton Conservative Association. The vote of thanks was seconded that evening by John Meikle. The constituency was won by the Conservatives three weeks later and remained in their hands until 1997.

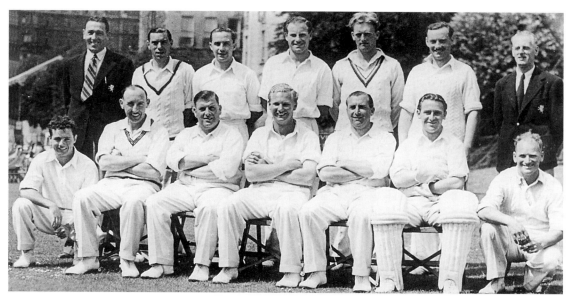

160 A classic Somerset team, photographed for Arthur Wellard's testimonial season, 1951. *Back row*: A. Wellard, E. Robinson, L. Angell, J. Redman, M. Tremlett, F. Irish, R. Trump (scorer). *Front row*: R. Smith, H. Buse, H. Hazell, S. Rogers (captain), H. Gimblett, H. Stephenson, J. Lawrence. The County Cricket Club came into being in 1875, and the County Ground at Taunton was acquired six years later.

TAUNTON DEANE entered the post-war era faced not only with continued rationing but with a severe shortage of housing. The reuniting of families and the decision of many wartime arrivals to remain in the district created a desperate need for accommodation, and not until the late 1950s did supply begin to meet demand. Abandoned army huts at the numerous camps around Taunton—including Culmhead, Courtlands and Sandhill Park—provided some families with temporary shelter. At first hundreds of enterprising squatters took over the huts, but later the buildings were treated as council property and rented out. Army huts at Sandhill Park were still occupied by at least 133 families as late as 1952, the year in which the government finally promised money to fund a corresponding number of new houses.

The local authorities of the Vale—Taunton Borough Council, Wellington Urban District Council, and the Rural District Councils of Taunton and Wellington—quickly embarked on house-building programmes which surpassed in scale even those of the 1920s and '30s. It was reported in December 1950 that Taunton RDC had built 196 houses since the end of the war, and more were in prospect at Norton Fitzwarren and Bishops Lydeard. In the same year Wellington RDC was building a council estate at Wiveliscombe, and planned smaller developments at Milverton, Fitzhead and Bradford on Tone. In Wellington itself work was under way on UDC developments at Longforth Road and Oaken Ground. But it was in Taunton that work progressed most rapidly. At the beginning of 1947 no fewer than 334 council houses were under construction in Holway, Priorswood and Wellsprings, and ten years later the completion of the 2,000th council house was a source of great civic pride. Such a rate of construction was made easier by the widespread use of prefabrication: the aluminium bungalows which long survived in Victory Road, for example, were each built in the course of a single working day and were ready for immediate occupation.

161 Evelyn Waugh, the most celebrated new resident to arrive in Taunton Deane during the 1950s. He acquired Combe Florey House in 1956 and died there 10 years later. The photograph shows him at Combe Florey in 1963.

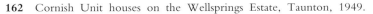

162 Cornish Unit houses on the Wellsprings Estate, Taunton, 1949.

The 'Plan for Taunton' devised by Thomas Sharp in 1946, and Somerset County Council's Development Plan of 1953, made detailed proposals for the town's future growth. Sharp's plan, including suggestions for inner and outer bypasses and the reclaiming of Castle Green as a dignified public space, was in general too ambitious for times of austerity. But both he and the County Council were agreed in their analysis of what Taunton had become. Though the town remained important as an agricultural market, as well as a local and regional shopping centre, it was now above all a centre of administration and of other services. That role had been confirmed in 1935 when the County Council's headquarters moved from Weston-super-Mare to Taunton, making Taunton beyond all doubt Somerset's county town, and by 1948 an employed population of almost 25,000 in the immediate area of Taunton contained 36 per cent who worked in public administration or professional services, and a further 21 per cent working in distributive trades or transport.

163   View of Taunton from St Mary's tower, *c.*1950.

164   Aerial view of County Hall and the Crescent, *c.*1950.

165   Aerial view of the Chelston junction of the M5 motorway, 1973.

Manufacturing industry, represented chiefly by the town's shirt and collar factories as well as by some recent arrivals such as Avimo, employed only 14 per cent, and was destined to decline yet further.

Infrastructure changes of the kind Sharp proposed came slowly to Taunton, and included the building of an inner bypass between 1959 and 1965 on a route which forced the sad destruction of part of Mary Street. Long-standing ambitions for an outer bypass, taking traffic on the A38 away from an increasingly congested town centre, were superseded in 1972 by an altogether grander civil engineering project: in that year construction of the Taunton section of the M5 motorway began, and four years later the route was complete between Exeter and Carlisle. Though Taunton was now spared the enormous volumes of summer traffic which had threatened to strangle it, the calm was deceptive; for the coming of the motorway heralded social, economic and physical changes perhaps more transforming than any that Taunton had ever experienced.

The new era began not only with the building of the motorway, but with a major redrawing of the local government map. Somerset County Council had come into existence in 1889 to perform many of the civil functions of Quarter Sessions, and the creation of rural and urban district councils followed six years later. On 1 April 1974, however, those longstanding arrangements were swept away. The County Council lost much of its northern territory to the new county of Avon, and the district councils in the Vale gave way to a single new authority soon called Taunton Deane Borough Council. The Deane Council was not a borough council in any historical sense, for its territory included much more than urban Taunton, gathering in Milverton, Wiveliscombe and Wellington—which resented its loss of independence—as well as a rural landscape reaching west to Raddington, east to Stoke St Gregory, north to Bagborough, and south to Otterford and Churchstanton.

By 1976 a series of ambitious road schemes was planned for Taunton, including a motorway link road, an eastern relief road, and a relief road crossing the railway at Silk Mills. Work on the schemes was completed in 1983 when Victoria Parkway and the Obridge viaduct came into use. Major commercial development was also under way. The Old Market Centre added 80,000 square feet of retail floor space to the town in 1982, the year in which the Asda superstore opened on Taunton's outskirts and exposed smaller food retailers to competitive pressures they found it increasingly difficult to withstand. In 1984, redevelopment of the area bounded by Billet Street and Silver Street began after long delays, and in 1985 three giant retail warehouses rose on a 10-acre site in Priory Fields, creating for the residents of Priory Avenue a night-time prospect likened by one of them to Las Vegas. The sale of Priory Fields brought the Borough Council some £3 million, a windfall which paid for the Deane House, the new Borough Council headquarters opened in 1987.

It was estimated that between 1980 and 1985 more than £43 million was spent in Taunton on commercial development and road schemes, a sum unmatched elsewhere in the South West other than in Bristol, and a sign of Taunton's hastening 'march towards regional status'. Few welcomed change unequivocally, and contending arguments were aired in the local press as well as in the council chamber. In 1985, Robert Smart of Pitminster wrote, 'If we are not careful, the planners will turn the town we love into a charmless, flat-fronted, hyper-efficient collection of computer-controlled, multi-national marketing outlets', while the Independent councillor, Rex Frost, asked, 'Does Taunton really want to become another Exeter or Bristol? Is there not merit in remaining what was often described as a sleepy old county town?' For John Meikle, Conservative leader of the Borough Council, the answer to such questions was simple. The development of Taunton was about creating jobs 'by encouraging new industry

166   The Princess of Wales in High Street, Taunton, during a visit in June 1993.

167   Drawing by Gwyneth Evans of the Market House, Taunton, following the reorganisation of the town centre in 1996.

and commerce, expanding the market and boosting tourism'.

Though the 1980s were a turning-point, the 1990s continued the process of radical transformation. Hankridge Farm, near the motorway junction, became the site of a new Sainsbury's superstore in 1992, and despite fierce opposition was soon growing into a major out-of-town retail complex, complete with a five-screen cinema. The Safeway superstore, near Taunton Market, was opened in 1993, and in 1996 the Town Centre Enhancement Scheme was completed. The scheme included the partial pedestrianisation of the area around the Market House, and despite some trenchant criticism—not least from Auberon Waugh—has generally been considered an aesthetic and practical success. Many small independent retailers finally vanished in this period, and areas where they had predominated, such as Station Road, were badly affected. But in general the 'rows of empty shops', predicted as early as 1982, have not become part of the street scene to the extent that some had feared. The economy has grown and the population with it. Taunton had a population of about 20,000 in 1901 and of about 34,000 in 1951; in 1998 it is estimated to contain 60,000 inhabitants out of a total population in Taunton Deane Borough of 100,000. Not all that multitude have prospered in the years of growth: the rapid widening of social inequalities during the '80s and '90s has been reflected locally in the return of beggars to Taunton streets, and the town's Halcon ward, developed with such idealistic hopes before the Second World War, has been identified as one of the most deprived areas in Somerset.

In the landscape around Taunton, the battles against development during the last 20 years have often been fought more fiercely than in the town itself. In the 1980s the people of Trull repeatedly opposed house-building plans which threatened to end the separation of their village from the town, and the inhabitants of Oake successfully objected at a public enquiry to a scheme for 65 houses (though a new

168   The dispossessed. Taff and Ferret under Castle Bow, August, 1998.

169   Loading sheep at Taunton Market, September 1998.

170   Villagers at Stoke St Mary gathered for a village photograph in August 1994.

scheme is now being built). But the tide of development and population growth will not easily be stemmed and in the twenty-year period to 2011 well over 10,000 new houses are likely to have been built in Taunton Deane, the majority focused on Taunton and Wellington. Within a generation Somerset's 'sleepy old county town'—essentially the town the Victorians created—will be no more than a distant memory, and our further impact on the rural landscape, in spite of all our care, will probably have been profound.

The years ahead will also decide the fate of the rural economy. The imminent closure by Matthew Clark Ltd. of the former Taunton Cider plant at Norton Fitzwarren has been felt with special force, not only because of the human consequences, but because large-scale commercial cider-making has provided until now a bond of continuity with the Vale's more traditional past. So too has farming, which in

1998 faces an economic crisis worse than any since the 1930s. Prices have collapsed, and many farmers, contending already with BSE as well as with the competing demands of environmental protection and the need to earn a living, have watched their incomes vanish. That the farming crisis as experienced in Taunton Deane has so little affected the great majority of its inhabitants would have seemed remarkable to earlier generations for whom the land lay near the heart of life, both practically and symbolically. Few now are directly dependent on local agriculture for a livelihood, and the feast of plenty so readily available in our superstores includes very little that is locally produced. As the millennium approaches, at the close of our calamitous and aspiring century, the great Vale of Taunton Deane has become little more than a setting for our lives. We have been made exiles from the landscape we inhabit, and may not quickly find a way home.

Select Bibliography

Acland, T.D. and Sturge, W., *The Farming of Somersetshire* (1851)

Allen, Gillian and Bush, Robin, *The Book of Wellington* (1981)

Arthurson, Ian, *The Perkin Warbeck Conspiracy, 1491-1499* (1994)

Bates, Rev. E.H. (ed.), *The Particular Description of the County of Somerset. Drawn up by Thomas Gerard of Trent*, 1633 (Somerset Record Society, vol. 15, 1900)

Bentley, J.B. and Murless, B.J., *Somerset Roads. The Legacy of the Turnpikes. Phase 1: Western Somerset* (1985)

Billingsley, John, *General View of the Agriculture of the County of Somerset* (1797)

Bush, R.J.E., 'The Tudor Tavern, Fore Street, Taunton', *Proceedings of the Somerset Archaeological and Natural History Society*, vol. 119 (1975)

Bush, Robin, *The Book of Taunton* (1977)

Bush, Robin, *Jeboult's Taunton* (1983)

Bush, Robin, *A Taunton Diary, 1787-1987* (1988)

Bushell, T.A., 'Somerset on Guard' (published in the *Somerset County Gazette*, 1950-51)

Clark, George Thomas, *Report to the General Board of Health, on a Preliminary Inquiry into ... the Sanitary Condition of the Inhabitants, of the Borough of Taunton* (1849)

Collinson, John, *The History and Antiquities of the County of Somerset* (3 vols, 1791)

Costen, Michael, *The Origins of Somerset* (1992)

Darby, H.C. and Finn, R. Welldon (eds), *The Domesday Geography of South-West England* (1967)

Dunning, Robert (ed.), *Christianity in Somerset* (1976)

Ellis, Peter, 'Norton Fitzwarren Hillfort: a Report on the Excavations by Nancy and Philip Langmaid between 1968 and 1971', *Proceedings of the Somerset Archaeological and Natural History Society*, vol. 133 (1989)

Farley, Frank E. and Ekless, Don F., *A History of Milverton* (1986)

Finberg, H.P.R., *The Early Charters of Wessex* (1964)

Fontaine, James, *Memoirs of a Huguenot Family* (1885, 1986)

Fox, H.S.A. and Thornton, C., 'Arable Productivity and Peasant Holdings at Taunton, 1209-1348' (unpublished ESRC research report, n.d.)

Grundy, G.B., *The Saxon Charters and Field Names of Somerset* (1935)

Guy, John R., *Malachi's Monument: the Taunton & Somerset Hospital at East Reach* (1986)

Haskell, Tony, *By Waterway to Taunton: a History of the Bridgwater and Taunton Canal and the River Tone Navigation* (1994)

Herbert, John Maurice and Page, Thomas, *Report ... on the Taunton Improvement and Market Bill* (1847)

Hugo, Thomas, *The History of Taunton Priory* (1860)

Hunt, T.J., *Ordination of the Vicarage of St Mary Magdalene, Taunton* (1958)

Hunt, T.J. (ed.), *The Medieval Customs of the Manors of Taunton and Bradford on Tone* (Somerset Record Society, vol. 66, 1962)

Kite, G.H. and Palmer, H.P., *Taunton, its History and Market Trust* (1926)

Leach, Peter (ed.), *The Archaeology of Taunton* (1980)

Marshall, William, *The Rural Economy of the West of England* (2 vols, 1796/1970)

Mayberry, Tom, *Orchard and the Portmans* (1986)

Mayberry, T.W., *Estate Records of the Bishops of Winchester in the Hampshire Record Office* (1988)

Reports of the Commissioners Appointed to Enquire Concerning Charities: Somersetshire, 1819-1837 (1894)

Rogers, Kenneth H., *Warp and Weft: the Somerset and Wiltshire Woollen Industry* (1986)

Royal Commission on the Employment of Children, Young Persons, and Women in Agriculture (1867): Report of Mr. R.F. Boyle on Somersetshire (1868-9)

Saffin, Eric, 'Another World: the Memories of Eric Saffin' (unpublished typescript, 1997)

Savage, J., *The History of Taunton* (1822)

Sharp, Thomas, *A Plan for Taunton* (1948)

Sixsmith, R.A., *Staple Fitzpaine and the Forest of Neroche* (1958)

Skeggs, James, 'Some Historic Gardens in Taunton Deane' (unpublished report for Taunton Deane Borough Council, 1994-5)

Somerset County Council, *County Development Plan 1953. Report of Survey Relating to the Taunton Area* (1953)

Somerset Federation of Women's Institutes, *Somerset Within Living Memory* (1992)

Somerset Record Society. In addition to volumes separately noted, key Record Society volumes include editions of registers of the bishops of Bath and Wells, 1309-1559 (13 vols), of Quarter Sessions records, 1607-76 (4 vols), and of wills, 1383-1558 (3 vols)

Stokes, James (ed.), *Records of Early English Drama: Somerset* (2 vols, 1996)

Thompson, W. Harding, *Somerset: Regional Survey* (1934)

Toulmin, Joshua, *The History of the Town of Taunton* (1791)

Weaver, Frederic William, *Wells Will* (1890)

Webb, Charles George, *The History of Taunton* (1874)

Weddell, P.J., *et al.*, 'Taunton Town Centre Enhancement Scheme 1996. Archaeological Recording and Excavation in Fore Street, The Parade and North Street' (unpublished report by Exeter Archaeology for Taunton Deane Borough Council, 1998)

White, Philip, *A Gentleman of Fine Taste: the Watercolours of Coplestone Warre Bampfylde* (1995)

Whitty, R.G. Hedworth, *The Court of Taunton in the 16th and 17th Centuries: a Study of Taunton under the Tudors and Stuarts* (1934)

Whitty, R.G. Hedworth, 'The History of Taunton under the Tudors and Stuarts' (unpublished PhD thesis, University of London, 1938)

Woolrich, A.P., 'The Taunton Waterworks Company, 1858-1877' (unpublished report for Wessex Water, 1996)

This book depends also on many archive and otherwise unpublished sources, including: (at the Somerset Record Office) 17th-century Quarter Sessions rolls; tithe maps and apportionments, 1837-42; copies of Edmund Rack's survey of Somerset, *c*.1785; and the research notes of T.J. Hunt on the manor of Taunton Deane; (at Somerset County Council's Environment and Property Department) the Sites and Monuments Record; (at the Hampshire Record Office) Pipe Rolls from 1208 for the estates of the bishopric of Winchester; and court rolls from 1507 for the manor of Taunton Deane.

Index

Figures in **bold** refer to illustration page numbers

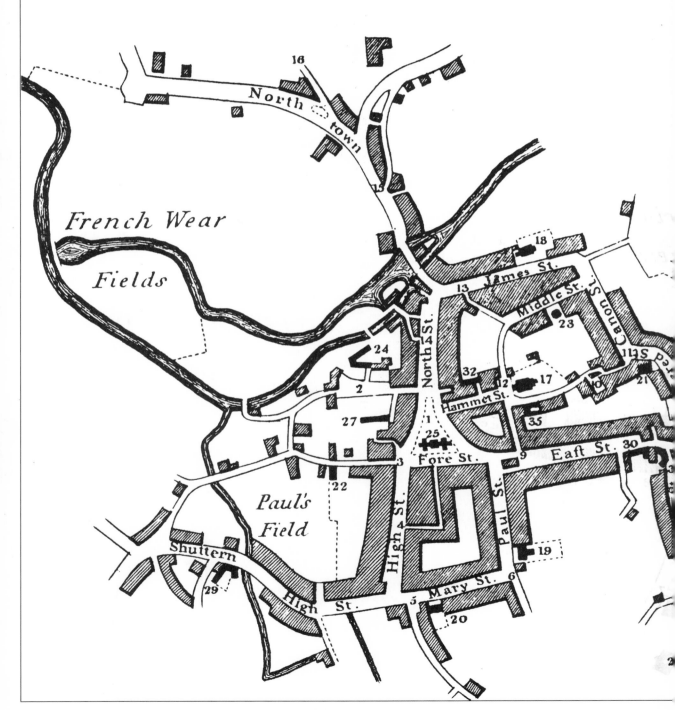

Map of Taunton, c.1790.